my **revisi⦿n** notes

WJEC and Eduqas GCSE

BUSINESS

David Salter

HODDER
EDUCATION
AN HACHETTE UK COMPANY

Orders: please contact Bookpoint Ltd, 130 Park Drive, Milton Park, Abingdon, Oxon OX14 4SE. Telephone: +44 (0)1235 827827. Fax: +44 (0)1235 400401. Email education@bookpoint.co.uk Lines are open from 9 a.m. to 5 p.m., Monday to Saturday, with a 24-hour message answering service. You can also order through our website: www.hoddereducation.co.uk

ISBN: 9781510426535
© David Salter 2018

First published in 2018 by
Hodder Education,
An Hachette UK Company
Carmelite House
50 Victoria Embankment
London EC4Y 0DZ

www.hoddereducation.co.uk

Impression number   10 9 8 7 6 5
Year   2022 2021

Cover photo © Rawpixel.com / Shutterstock
Illustrations by Integra Software Serv. LTD.
Typeset in India by Integra Software Serv. LTD.
Printed in India

A catalogue record for this title is available from the British Library.

MIX
Paper from
responsible sources
FSC™ C104740

Get the most from this book

Everyone has to decide his or her own revision strategy, but it is essential to review your work, learn it and test your understanding. These Revision Notes will help you to do that in a planned way, topic by topic. Use this book as the cornerstone of your revision and don't hesitate to write in it – personalise your notes and check your progress by ticking off each section as you revise.

Tick to track your progress

Use the revision planner on pages 4 and 5 to plan your revision, topic by topic. Tick each box when you have:

● revised and understood a topic
● tested yourself
● practised the exam questions and gone online to check your answers.

You can also keep track of your revision by ticking off each topic heading in the book. You may find it

helpful to add your own notes as you work through each topic.

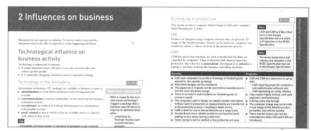

Features to help you succeed

Key terms

Clear, concise definitions of essential key terms are provided where they first appear.

Now test yourself

These short, knowledge-based questions provide the first step in testing your learning. Answers are online.

Exam practice

Practice exam questions are provided for each topic. Use them to consolidate your revision and practise your exam skills.

Tips

Expert tips are given to help you polish your exam technique in order to maximise your chances in the exam.

Online

Go online to see answers to the 'Now test yourself' and 'Exam practice' questions. You will find these at **www.hoddereducation.co.uk/ myrevisionnotesdownloads**

Notes

These notes highlight any differences between the content covered by the WJEC and Eduqas specifications so that you know which material you need to revise for your exam.

My revision planner

REVISED   TESTED   EXAM READY

<table>
<tr><td></td><td>REVISED</td><td>TESTED</td><td>EXAM READY</td></tr>
</table>

5 Marketing

6 Human resources

Exam practice questions

Answers to Now test yourself and Exam-style questions online at www.hoddereducation.co.uk/myrevisionnotesdownloads

4 - paper 1   4 - paper 2
19 topics   16 topics

topics not being studied at all:
- business enterprise
- business location & site
- the interdependant nature of business
- the impact of legislation on businesses
- the supply chain
- sources of finance
- cash flow
- organisational structure

topics for both papers:
- the nature of business activity   - training
- business aims and objectives
- business growth
- revenue and costs
- financial performance
- promotion
- place

Countdown to my exams

6–8 weeks to go

- Start by looking at the specification – make sure you know exactly what material you need to revise and the style of the examination. Use the revision planner on pages 4 and 5 to familiarise yourself with the topics.
- Organise your notes, making sure you have covered everything on the specification. The revision planner will help you to group your notes into topics.
- Work out a realistic revision plan that will allow you time for relaxation. Set aside days and times for all the subjects that you need to study, and stick to your timetable.
- Set yourself sensible targets. Break your revision down into focused sessions of around 40 minutes, divided by breaks. These Revision Notes organise the basic facts into short, memorable sections to make revising easier.

REVISED

2–6 weeks to go

- Read through the relevant sections of this book and refer to the tips and key terms. Tick off the topics as you feel confident about them. Highlight those topics you find difficult and look at them again in detail.
- Test your understanding of each topic by working through the 'Now test yourself' questions in the book. Look up the answers online at: **www.hoddereducation.co.uk/ myrevisionnotesdownloads**
- Make a note of any problem areas as you revise, and ask your teacher to go over these in class.
- Look at past papers. They are one of the best ways to revise and practise your exam skills. Write or prepare planned answers to the exam practice questions provided in this book. Check your answers online at **www.hoddereducation. co.uk/myrevisionnotesdownloads**
- Track your progress using the revision planner and give yourself a reward when you have achieved your target.

REVISED

One week to go

- Try to fit in at least one more timed practice of an entire past paper and seek feedback from your teacher, comparing your work closely with the mark scheme.
- Check the revision planner to make sure you haven't missed out any topics. Brush up on any areas of difficulty by talking them over with a friend or getting help from your teacher.
- Attend any revision classes put on by your teacher. Remember, he or she is an expert at preparing people for examinations.

REVISED

The day before the examination

- Flick through these Revision Notes for useful reminders, for example the key terms.
- Check the time and place of your examination.
- Make sure you have everything you need – extra pens and pencils, tissues, a watch, bottled water, sweets.
- Allow some time to relax and have an early night to ensure you are fresh and alert for the examination.

REVISED

My exams

Paper 1

Date:...

Time:...

Location:...

Paper 2

Date:...

Time:...

Location:...

1 Business activity

The nature of business activity

What is a business?

REVISED

It is an organisation that produces goods and services. For most the main aim is to earn profits for the owners. To do this it needs to be able to buy resources from suppliers at a cost and to sell these on, in a changed form, to its customers.

Businesses:
- operate in a **competitive** environment. There are other businesses producing the same or similar goods and each is trying to gain customers from all other businesses
- operate in a **dynamic** environment. The business world is always changing. Competitors are producing new products, while customers demand different goods and services
- need to **identify and respond** to this dynamic environment and to the business opportunities created
- need to **appreciate** the consequences and opportunities of operating at different scales, for example in local, national or global markets
- are **interdependent**. They rely on other businesses for their materials or as their customers. This interdependence also applies within a business, where the actions in one part of the business affect the outcomes in another.

Providing goods and services

Goods and services

REVISED

Goods are products that can be seen, touched and handled. There are two types of goods:
1 **Consumer goods**, which are those used by the final user. These goods may be divided into **durable goods** and **non-durable goods**.
2 **Producer goods**, which are products bought by a company and used to produce other goods and services.

Services are provided for individuals and businesses: they are offered to or for their customers. The two types of services are **personal** and **commercial**.

Durable goods are consumer goods that are not used at once and do not have to be bought frequently because they last for a long time.

Non-durable goods are goods that are immediately consumed or that have a lifespan of less than three years.

Personal services are those services provided for individuals. They include services for personal grooming, house maintenance, car repair, etc.

Commercial services are services that provide mainly to businesses such as transport and warehousing, but they may also be available to individuals such as insurance and banking.

The private and the public sectors

All goods and services need to be produced. The organisations that provide these may be in:

- **the private sector**
  Made up of businesses set up by individuals or groups that produce goods and services to sell to others to make a profit. Most goods and services in the United Kingdom are provided by the private sector in the form of sole traders, partnerships and limited companies.
- **the public sector**
  Sometimes the private sector is not willing to provide certain goods and services (which might include education, health for all or environmental services), or won't provide them at a price people are willing to pay. Such products will instead be provided by the public sector, which is made up of businesses owned and operated by government organisations at national, regional or local level.

p & shareholders

> **Private sector** organisations are owned by individuals.
>
> **Public sector** organisations are owned by the government.

> **Tip**
>
> Do not confuse the private and public sectors with private and public companies.

Resources needed to produce goods and services

Businesses combine resources to produce goods and services. These resources include:

- raw materials such as coal or wood
- machinery, equipment and buildings
- workers in sufficient numbers with the right skills, qualifications and experience
- a site on which to build the factory, shop or office.

Now test yourself

1 Suggest two ways in which businesses may compete.
2 Suggest two differences between durable and non-durable goods.
3 Give one example of a personal service and one of a commercial service.
4 Give two examples of services that are provided by both the private and public sectors.

1) price & quality

2) durable : long lasting, not used at once
   non-durable : less than 3 years, can be used at once.

3) personal service : hairdresser
   commercial service : logistics (transport)

4)

resources : land, labour, capital, enterprise

Business enterprise

What is business enterprise? REVISED

Business enterprise involves an individual or group of individuals realising that there is an opportunity to set up a business. This may come about because:
- they see a gap in the market for a new product
- they see others earning profits in providing a good or service and believe they can do the same.

Once the business has been set up they will continue to own and to run the business. A person who carries out business enterprise is known as an **entrepreneur**.

> An **entrepreneur** is a person who sets up a business and is willing to take on financial risks in the hope of making a profit.

The role of the entrepreneur in business activity REVISED

The entrepreneur has many roles and functions in setting up and running a business:
- showing **initiative** by spotting an opportunity, reacting quickly to change, and having the skills and enthusiasm to set up a business based upon this
- having the **innovation** to stay ahead of the competition by developing new products

- **identifying opportunities** in new and existing markets
- **organising resources** to get the best out of suppliers and workers, to ensure that goods and services are produced for customers.

The characteristics of an entrepreneur REVISED

The roles and functions of an entrepreneur, looked at previously, can also be thought of as some of an entrepreneur's key characteristics. An entrepreneur will have a range of additional qualities that must combine to ensure the success of the business. These additional characteristics include being:
- a **risk taker**. Many new businesses close within their first year: entrepreneurs will take the risk in the hope that they succeed

- a **decision maker**. The success of the business may require fast decisions based on the evidence and sensible business choices
- **hardworking**. This may involve long hours to run the business
- **determined** to try to make the business succeed.

The motives of entrepreneurs REVISED

Why do some people become entrepreneurs?

Financial reasons

Money is an important motivator. An entrepreneur might want:
- to earn an **income** after becoming unemployed
- to earn a **profit**, which may be greater than their income when working for someone else.

Non-financial reasons

These include:
- Some entrepreneurs want to be their **own boss** and make all the decisions regarding the business.
- Running a business can provide **personal satisfaction**.

- Some business owners want to continue **family businesses**.
- Being an entrepreneur provides the opportunity for business owners to earn a living from a **hobby or interest**.

Social or community reasons

Some businesses are set up primarily for the benefit of the local community, for example a local community shop, an electricity-generating scheme or a charity shop. Such businesses are called **social enterprises**.

> **Social enterprises** are businesses that operate for the benefit of the community or its workers or as a charity.

The risks and rewards of business enterprise

Is it a good idea for someone to want to become an entrepreneur? To answer this question you must consider the risks and rewards.

Risks

Some of the problems faced by an entrepreneur might include:
- The business may have lower than expected sales because:
  - customers might prefer the products of a competitor
  - the business may have received bad publicity
  - the incomes of buyers might have fallen.
- Unexpected increases in the costs of materials, wage bills or taxes might result in the business paying out more money than was planned for.
- Unexpected events such as a damaging storm or traffic jams might delay production, increase costs and reduce sales.

Any of these issues might lead to a worsening of standards of living for the entrepreneur, or even the collapse of the business.

Rewards

The benefits for the entrepreneur might include:
- Entrepreneurs can earn more from the profits of their businesses than they would earn working for someone else.
- The satisfaction gained from owning and running your own business; of being the boss and making the decisions.
- Building something new, developing your own products or services and having your name on the goods or over the shop.
- Positive customer feedback and building good relationships with those who buy your goods or receive your services.

Advice and help to an entrepreneur

The owner of a new business start-up may not know much about setting up or running their own enterprise. There are several sources of help, support and advice to such entrepreneurs.
- The **Welsh Government** supports new and established enterprises to develop and grow. It provides advice on business plans, raising finance, marketing and e-commerce. The **Business Wales** website includes advice, case studies about other entrepreneurs, a business directory and details about courses and websites.
- There are many **advice websites** for small businesses online. Some offer free help while others are linked to financial organisations that are looking to invest in new businesses.
- **Commercial banks** provide advice in bank branches, start-up guides, loans and short-term free business banking.
- Independent help is available from the young person's charity, the **Prince's Trust**. Their Enterprise Programme helps anyone aged 18–30 set up their own business. Assistance involves advice on business-related matters, mentoring of young entrepreneurs and a loan of up to £5000.

> **Note**
>
> This section only applies to the WJEC Specification – not to the Eduqas Specification.

> **Tip**
>
> In questions where you are asked to 'Outline', write one sentence to answer the question and at least one more to explain what you have written.

Now test yourself

1 Describe three of the most important characteristics of being an entrepreneur.
2 Outline a non-financial reason for wanting to be an entrepreneur.
3 Suggest two risks faced by entrepreneurs.
4 Apart from profits, describe one benefit of being an entrepreneur.

Business planning

Is business planning important?

Business planning helps show what skills and capital a business has, and to decide how these can be used most effectively. It is very important that entrepreneurs and new businesses write a **business plan**, but it is also essential for established businesses to do this as well.

The role of a business plan in a start-up

- As a **decision-making tool**. It helps the potential entrepreneur decide whether to set up a business or not. It analyses the important factors needed to set up and to run the business so the individual can make clearly thought out, sensible decisions.
- When **seeking finance or investment**. Before others will provide money for the business, they will need to know that all financial issues have been investigated.
- Showing **future vision**. It helps to show the future plans for the business, making it clear that it is a dynamic business.
- As a **management tool**. It helps the business by showing employees the aims that everyone should be working towards.

> A **business plan** sets out what the business does at present, plus what it intends to achieve in the future and how this will be accomplished. The plan will include marketing and financial plans.

What is included in a business plan?

This is up to the entrepreneur but banks will want to see certain features if they are to provide loans. These will include:

- **Business description**, to include details such as:
  - its name
  - the type of ownership – is it a sole trader or a limited company?
  - the type of goods it sells or the services it provides. Banks will have data on the chances of success of types of business in an area.
- **Marketing**. What marketing plans does the business have?
  - Has it carried out market research?
  - What were the results of the market research?
  - What plans does it have for location or price or promotion?
- **Financial**. What financial information does the business have? For new businesses, this might be a cash-flow forecast and for existing businesses a profit and loss account.
- **Production operations** of the business, for example:
  - how and where the goods will be produced
  - the scale of operation
  - whether resources will need to be imported.
- **Human resources**. What are the human resource requirements of the business?
  - How many workers will be needed?
  - Will they be skilled or unskilled?
  - What will be the level of wages and salaries?

how to forecast revenue as a new business?

- forecast number of customers per day.

- forecast an average spend per visit.

1 What is a business plan?
2 Why will banks need to know the type of ownership of a business?
3 Which two items of financial information would banks consider essential in a business plan?
4 Why it is important to the entrepreneur to have a business plan?

Business aims and objectives

What are business aims?

Business aims are the long-term goals of the business. These may include:
- **Survival**. The owners want the business to continue into the long term. This will provide them with employment, income and something to pass on to family.
- **Profit maximisation**. Many owners want to make as much profit as possible given the size of the business and its market.
- **Growth**. Most large businesses started as small enterprises. Entrepreneurs setting up businesses today will aim to grow their businesses as time passes.
- **Market share**. This involves the entrepreneur wanting to have the highest percentage of customers as possible and perhaps to be the biggest business in the market.
- **Customer satisfaction** is important to business. Many will provide feedback forms and customer satisfaction surveys. Good results in these will please the entrepreneur.
- **Social and community** aims mean that some businesses want to make a good impression in the community. They may sponsor local sports teams or musical events.
- **Ethical and environmental** aims are important to some.
  - Businesses that are ethically motivated want to do the right thing for their suppliers, their workers and their customers.
  - Businesses with environmental concerns attempt to run their enterprises without doing harm to the world around them.

> **Business aims** are general goals for a business.
>
> A **business objective** is a specific target that is set for a business to achieve its aim.

> **Tip**
>
> Do not assume that market share is just about the size of revenue or sales or profit. It is about the percentage of sales one firm has in the entire market.

any three:
- survival
- growth
- customer satisfaction

The role of business objectives

Business objectives are targets set by businesses. Their targets help them in the day-to-day management and decision making of the business, and also to measure the performance of the businesses.

SMART objectives

To better help them meet their targets, a business's objectives should be **SMART**.
- **S**pecific. The objective must be precise. It is not enough to say that the entrepreneur wants the business to grow. The objective could relate to growth in sales, revenue, profit, number of shops or number of employees.
- **M**easurable. The objective should involve a number or a percentage as a target.
- **A**greed by all the relevant stakeholders. This helps ensure everyone involved in the business is working towards the same objective.
- **R**ealistic or achievable. It must be possible to reach the objective.
- **T**imed, so that everyone will know when the objective has been reached.

- specific
- measurable
- agreed
- realistic
- timed

Different aims and objectives for different business

The aims and objectives of each business will vary depending on the size, age and purpose of the business, as well as the personal aims of the entrepreneur. However, speaking generally, new businesses will tend to be small and focused primarily on just surviving the early years of the business. Established small businesses may want to concentrate on earning enough profits to maintain the entrepreneur and their family, and/or satisfy the social and material needs of their customers and local community. Large businesses will usually aim to maximise profits to:

- grow the business
- increase market share
- pay the dividends of their shareholders
- earn bonuses for their managers.

Changing business aims

A competitive and dynamic business environment means that aims and objectives may need to be changed. This could be because of internal or external factors.

Internal

Events within the business may require the owners to reconsider the objectives, for example:

- faster or slower growth than expected
- greater or less profit than expected
- reaching objectives earlier than expected.

External

Events outside the business may lead to a reconsideration of objectives, for example:

- a change in consumer incomes
- changes in government policy and taxation
- economic factors such as changes in interest rates.

Now test yourself

1 Why is profit maximisation important for growth and survival?
2 What is meant by the term market share?
3 Suggest two features that can be measured to show the growth of a business.
4 How will an increase in consumer incomes change the targets set by a business?

Stakeholders and business

The main **stakeholders** are:

- **Owners**. In limited companies, these are the shareholders. They will be concerned about their dividends and the value of their shares.
- **Employees**, who will be affected by changes in wages and salaries and working conditions.
- **Managers**, who are employees of the business and will be concerned about their pay, conditions, and their status and responsibilities.
- **Customers**, who expect to receive the best quality products at the most appropriate prices.
- **Suppliers**, who provide materials and services to the business. They are concerned that they provide quality products in the right quantities and that they receive prompt payment for the goods supplied.
- **Government**, which relies on businesses as they provide employment and pay taxes. It also passes laws to ensure that workers are treated properly and that products are of appropriate quality for consumers.
- **Local communities** want businesses to provide jobs for their areas and to ensure that environmental conditions are met.

Stakeholders are individuals and organisations that affect and are affected by the activities of a business.

How stakeholders influence businesses and the impact of business aims and objectives on stakeholders

Stakeholders are affected by business and they can also affect how businesses operate. This can be seen in:
- decision making
- aims and objectives
- operational issues
- sales, costs and profits.

For example, a business may be considering expanding a factory. The planning and decision will be based on existing aims and objectives and will affect how the business operates and its sales, costs and profits. The outcome will depend on inputs from owners, employees, the government and local communities.

The expanded factory will impact on all stakeholders to varying degrees. Due to the number of different stakeholders, all with different aims and priorities, there is likely to be disagreement between them. Potential areas of conflict include: maximising profit, low wages, environmental damage, poor quality products and late payment for materials. Some stakeholders will gain while others will lose, for example:

Stakeholder	Positive	Negative	Area of impact
Owners/shareholders	Greater long-term output and, they hope, profit	May see a short-term fall in their dividends (used to pay for the expansion)	Financial
Employees/managers	May see an improvement in working conditions and in promotional opportunities	Improvements may result in new technology, which puts their jobs at risk	Employment
Customers	May see an increase in the number of goods available, possibly at lower prices	The cost of the expansion may need to be paid for with higher prices	Products and services
Suppliers	May be called upon to supply more materials	The factory expansion might impact cash flow, so suppliers may face late payments	Operational
Local, regional and national governments	Potential increase in employment opportunities and extra tax income from business/employees	May be asked to provide grants for the expansion and face requests to improve the infrastructure	Financial/employment
Local communities	May see more job opportunities and an improved infrastructure	May be an increase in pollution and congestion	Products and services/social

Now test yourself

1 What role will the local community play when a business is planning to expand a factory?
2 Describe two ways in which the employees will be affected by decisions made by the owners.
3 Suggest two stakeholders who might be in favour of an objective to increase output.
4 Which stakeholders would be affected by a decision to introduce new machinery?

Business ownership

Unlimited liability businesses

Two businesses with **unlimited liability** are **sole traders** and **partnerships**.

Sole traders

Benefits	Problems
● Easy and cheap to set up because they are established by one person, and there are few formalities. ● All decisions are made by the owner without consultation, and so without delay. This independence means sole traders can work when they want and at their own pace. ● All profits can be kept by the owner. ● Affairs can be kept private so there is no need to publish accounts. ● The sole trader will often have good relations with customers and employees, so personal services can be provided.	● Owner has unlimited liability. ● There is no continuity so, if the sole trader leaves the business, it will come to an end. ● Limited capital when the business is being set up, and when it is in operation. ● The workload and responsibilities of owning and running a business can be great. ● Decisions made by the sole trader can be rushed and poorly thought through.

Partnerships

Many entrepreneurs forming a partnership agree to a **Deed of Partnership**.

Benefits	Problems
● Relatively easy to set up. No legal agreement is needed, but many will sign a Deed of Partnership. ● All profits belong to the partners. ● Affairs can be kept private so there is no need to publish accounts nor give details of the ownership. ● The partners will have good relations with customers and employees so personal services can be provided. ● Partnerships are usually able to raise more capital than sole traders. ● Different partners contribute different skills and expertise to the business. ● Partnerships have more people to make decisions, so there is likely to be a more considered approach to running the business.	● The partners have unlimited liability. ● There is limited continuity so, if one partner leaves, the business may come to an end. ● Partners may disagree on the operation of the business. This means decisions will take longer to reach. ● Some partners may not work as hard as others. The share of profit they receive may feel undeserved, which can be demoralising and may cause arguments. ● Despite being able to raise more finance than sole traders, there may still be limited capital.

Unlimited liability occurs when the personal possessions of the owners of the business are at risk if there are any problems. There is no limit to the amount of money the owners may have to pay out.

A **sole trader** is an individual who sets up in business on his or her own.

Partnerships are businesses owned by two or more people.

A **Deed of Partnership** is an agreement between partners that sets out the rules of the partnership, such as how profits will be divided and how the partnership will be valued if someone wants to leave.

Tip

Do not assume that sole traders work alone. They can employ other people but they are the only owners of the business.

Now test yourself

1 What is meant by the term unlimited liability?
2 Suggest three ways in which the capital of sole traders and of partnerships may be limited.
3 Why should people planning to set up a partnership agree to a Deed of Partnership?
4 Suggest two advantages partnerships have over sole trader businesses.

TESTED

Limited liability businesses

Limited liability businesses are owned by at least two shareholders. They are run by a Board of Directors elected at the Annual General Meeting by the shareholders. Two businesses with limited liability are private limited companies and public limited companies.

Private limited companies

Benefits	Problems
• The shareholders have limited liability. • They have a separate corporate identity, so the shareholders are not responsible for the actions of the company. • The business has continuity, so if shareholders sell their shares, the business will not end. • They will have more capital than unlimited liability businesses as they can sell shares. • Companies can gain from specialised management employed by the Board of Directors.	• May be expensive and difficult to organise as a range of documents is needed to ensure the business is set up and managed properly and legally. • Profits are shared with shareholders. This payment is known as the **dividend**. • The affairs of the private limited company are not private. The business must publish an annual report outlining the progress of the business including its detailed accounts. • Capital may be limited as money cannot be raised from investors on the Stock Exchange.

Public limited companies

The advantages and disadvantages of a **public limited company** are the same as a private limited company, but they also have additional advantages and disadvantages over other types of business ownership.

Benefits	Problems
• They have more access to capital as they are able to sell shares to the public on the Stock Exchange. • Banks are more likely to lend them more money, often at lower rates of interest. • Public limited companies are the best-known businesses. This not only encourages greater share ownership in them but consumers also have more confidence in buying from them.	• As shares are available to anyone on the Stock Exchange, there is the possibility of the owners losing control of business (if someone takes control of more than half the shares). • The business's accounts must be made available to anyone who is interested, so are not likely to remain private, and may be reported on in the media. • It is expensive to set up and run a public limited company. More documents are needed to establish the business, and contacting shareholders also costs a great deal. • Owners do not have to spend their time with the day-to-day management of the business, so there is said to be a divorce of the ownership and control of the business.

Limited liability occurs when there is a limit to the amount of money investors can lose; they can only lose the funds invested and not their personal possessions.

A **private limited company** cannot publicly advertise its shares for sale and is often owned by family members. Private limited companies are generally recognised by having **and Company Ltd** following their names.

A **public limited company** can advertise its shares and can be listed on the Stock Exchange. Public limited companies are generally recognised by having **plc** following their names.

Tip

Remember it is the owners of the business who have limited liability, not the business.

Tip

There is no need to know how companies are set up nor about the documents involved.

Now test yourself

1 Outline the main advantage of limited liability to shareholders.
2 How do businesses benefit from having limited liability?
3 What is meant by separate legal identity?
4 What is the main advantage public limited companies have over private limited companies?

TESTED

Other types of business

Co-operatives

The aim of **co-operatives** is to earn a profit. This profit is distributed to its members rather than to the owners and shareholders.

> A **co-operative** exists when a business is owned and run by its members.
>
> A **charity** is a non-profit-making organisation that is set up for 'charitable purposes'.

Worker co-operatives

A worker co-operative is a business that is owned and controlled by its workers. There are about 1500 worker co-operatives in the United Kingdom. Some were set up by the workers taking over from the previous owners perhaps because of the possibility of the business closing: this helped these workers to keep their jobs. The main features are:

● Workers invest money in the business, but this investment may be as little as £1.
● All workers play a part in making decisions so:
  ○ they share the risks but also
  ○ they share the profits as well as earning their wages as employees.

Consumer co-operatives

These are the most common type of co-operative. They have been involved in retailing, banking, travel agents and funeral directors. The main features are:

● A consumer co-operative is owned by its customers.
● They pay a subscription, often of just £1, to become members.
● Members receive a share of the profits, which is based on the value of goods bought.

Benefits	Problems
● Because they are involved with the running of the business, co-operative members are motivated to work for, or shop at, the business. ● Profits are not the only objective. Customer service is important, as are ethical issues such as the treatment of workers, suppliers and society in general. ● Profits are distributed fairly among the members. ● Workers who share the same aims and objectives all work for the benefit of the business and are less likely to argue. ● Worker co-operatives are involved in the education and training of employees.	● Decisions may take a long time as everybody has a say in the running of the business. Most co-operatives employ managers to make day-to-day decisions (informed by the aims and objectives of the co-operative). ● They may find it difficult to recruit the best managers, as the most able usually demand high salaries, which the members of co-operatives are unwilling to pay. ● Co-operative owners generally have no experience of running a business. ● Without business experience, making tough decisions that affect their fellow workers, such as job cuts, is much harder. ● The dominance of ethical considerations may mean the business is not focused on maximised profits or growth.

Charities

Charities are not often seen as businesses but, as they provide goods and services to make a profit, they need to be included. Their aim is to minimise costs and to organise fundraising events. Any profits are used to benefit their charitable cause. To ensure this happens, decisions are made by trustees.

Workers may be employed to manage the charities and their events, but wage costs are kept to a minimum by relying on volunteers.

Now test yourself

1 Who are most likely to be the owners of co-operative shops?
2 Charities are said to be non-profit organisations. Why do they still aim to make a profit?

Business growth

Why businesses grow

Businesses aim to grow for a number of reasons:
- To **increase profits**.
- They hope to **reduce competition**, which will also help them to **improve their market share**.
- Bigger firms are also more able to **diversify**, to **spread risks**.
- Larger business can gain the benefits of **internal economies of scale**.

Internal economies of scale

- **Purchasing** economies of scale mean large businesses can negotiate lower prices for materials because they bulk buy.

- **Marketing** economies mean larger firms can afford a higher advertising budget than smaller businesses, but the cost can be spread over the increase in sales from the advertising.
- **Technical** economies mean larger firms are more able to afford modern equipment and to pay for this with increased output.
- **Financial** economies mean large businesses can negotiate lower rates of interest with the banks for the vast sums of money they borrow.
- **Administrative** economies mean large businesses can afford to pay the highest salaries for managers to run the business efficiently and profitably.

How do businesses grow?

Businesses grow by selling more products and earning more revenue in existing markets and by diversifying.

Successful growth will depend on:
- spending on market research, product development and investment in new factories and equipment
- increased advertising and sales promotions.

Internal (organic) growth

Internal or organic growth happens within the business by:
- **selling more** in existing markets
- searching for **new markets** at home and abroad
- developing and launching **new products**
- increasing **promotion** and **investment**.

The benefits of **diversification** include:
- competing in different markets, so increasing total sales revenue in the hope of earning greater profits
- operating in different markets to spread the risks across the range of products it produces
- a better reputation and increased customer loyalty.

External growth (integration)

External growth happens when businesses grow by:
- combining with other businesses (this is a **merger**) or
- acquiring – or buying – other businesses (this is a **takeover**).

The mergers or takeovers involve either **horizontal integration** or **vertical integration**.

Vertical integration can be done in two distinct ways.

1 **Backward integration** is when a business buys one of its suppliers.
2 **Forward integration** is when a business buys a company to which they previously sold their products.

Economies of scale occur when the cost per unit falls as a business expands.

Internal or organic growth is where a business grows by selling more of its own products.

Diversification is when a business sells new products in new markets.

External growth is where a business grows by joining with another business.

Horizontal integration is where a business joins with another at the same stage of the production process.

Vertical integration is where a business joins with another at a different stage of the same production process.

Tip

There is no need to know about external economies of scale nor dis-economies of scale.

Now test yourself

1 Which term is used for a company that takes over one of its suppliers of raw materials?
2 What do you understand by the terms (a) acquisitions and (b) internal growth?

Evaluation of integration

The benefits and problems of integration depend upon the type of business and the stakeholders involved. For some, the higher profits and wider market might be an advantage but, for others, the reduced number of suppliers might be a disadvantage.

Stakeholder	Benefits	Problems
The business	● An improved corporate image as the business is now found in several sectors. ● Joint advertising can promote all goods and services produced. ● Greater control over price as there's less worry about competitor pricing. ● Following vertical integration, the business has greater control over the supply of factors of production, and of costs. ● Can keep the profits at each level of production.	● A much larger business may need to be organised and managed in a different way.
Owners	● Economies of scale may lead to greater profits for the business and returns for the owners.	● There may be more shares in the expanded company, so the price of shares may fall, reducing the value of the owner's stock.
Employees	● Those who remain with the businesses may receive higher incomes. ● The larger firm may provide more responsible posts and offer better prospects for promotion.	● There may be job losses, particularly in the business being taken over. ● Workers may be asked to relocate to a different area to keep their jobs, creating a negative impact on family and housing. ● Workers may have to re-apply for their jobs.
Managers	● Same as employee benefits.	● Same as employee problems.
Customers	● May enjoy lower prices if the economies of scale benefits are passed on.	● The number of locations where customers can buy goods and services may reduce, and prices may increase.
Suppliers	● May have a more secure market, with the larger business better able to cope with competition and pay for resources.	● The new large business will have a greater control over suppliers, which might affect their prices, their sales and the amount of money they receive.
Government	● Higher profits will lead to more taxes being paid. ● An internationally competitive business strengthens the international trading position of its country. ● Higher worker salaries could lead to higher income tax being paid.	● If workers lose their jobs, more benefits may need to be paid.
Local people	● Older, less efficient factories may be closed, so reducing pollution and congestion in some areas.	● Might find bigger neighbour factories with more pollution and congestion.

Now test yourself

TESTED

1 Outline one way in which businesses benefit from integration.
2 Does the Government always benefit from integration? Explain your answer.
3 Suggest one effect that integration might have on the environment.
4 Describe one effect on the workers of a factory taken over by another business.

Franchising

Franchising is a method of growth for the established business (the **franchisor**), who sells the person buying the franchise (the **franchisee**) the right to use the name and methods of their established business, so that they might reproduce the success of the business in another location.

> **Franchising** is paying a franchise owner to open an established business.
>
> A **franchisor** sells the franchise to the franchisee.
>
> A **franchisee** buys the franchise from the franchisor.

> **Tip**
>
> A franchise is not a type of business ownership. Businesses involved in franchises can be sole traders or partnerships or limited companies. Franchises cannot be compared with any of these. Do not confuse franchisor and franchisee. No marks will be gained if you write about the wrong one.

Advantages and disadvantages of franchises

Franchisor benefits	Franchisor problems

• Receives **royalty** payments from the franchisee, for the right to use the businesses name and methods.
• The business grows without the franchisor doing much of the work required.
• The franchisor **sells stock** to the franchisee. This ensures all products sold across the franchise are the same.
• A new franchisee may have more **enthusiasm** than a long-term manager to help the franchise to succeed.
• The franchisee finds the location, organises planning permission and pays the rent and for the fittings. This lowers costs for the franchisor.
• The franchisee recruits the **workforce**, pays the wages and complies with employment law.
	• The franchisor pays some of the franchise **costs**:
	  – Training costs, to ensure the franchisee and workers are up to the franchisor's standard.
	  – National advertising costs.
	  – Costs related to the organisation and design of the outlet.
	• The franchisor has **less control** over outlets, as day-to-day running is carried out by the franchisees.
	• The franchisor may suffer if an outlet is **badly run** by a franchisee.

Franchisee benefits	Franchisee problems

• The well-known name of the franchisor will mean **more customers** for the franchisee.
• Receives **advice and training** from the franchisor.
• **National advertising**, paid for by the franchisor, will make the franchise better known.
• Furniture and fittings may be provided by the franchisor to provide a corporate image for and a **standard quality** across the franchise.
• **Loans and finance** may be provided by the franchisor at favourable rates of interest.
• Each franchisee is given **exclusive rights** within an area, so reducing the competition.
• The franchisor provides the **goods to sell**, so there is no need to find suppliers.
	• A **set-up cost** is paid to the franchisor to join the franchise.
	• **Royalties** are paid by the franchisee. These are an additional cost to the business.
	• Goods, which must be bought from the franchisor, may be **more expensive** than from other suppliers.
	• The franchisee has **little influence** over:
	  – the design of the outlet
	  – the goods sold
	  – the area in which they are sold.
	• The franchisee may suffer from the **bad reputation** of other franchisees.

Now test yourself

1 Which type of business allows others to use its name in return for royalty payments?
2 Describe one advantage and one disadvantage of a business offering franchises.
3 Explain two advantages a sole trader might gain from joining a franchise.
4 Outline two ways in which belonging to a franchise might add to costs for a franchisee.

Why do some businesses remain small?

Most enterprises, even the largest corporations of today, started as small businesses. The owners of these small businesses aim for growth, but it takes time.

The aim of many businesses is to grow but most businesses are, or remain, small. Why is this?

- The **market size may be limited**, for example:
  - geographically. There are many convenience and village stores that sell goods in local communities: these are unlikely to grow, as they are limited by the size of the local community that they serve. Many supermarket chains are now recognising the local market and are opening smaller, local convenience stores.
  - in terms of product. Some goods and services can only be supplied on a small scale, for example those provided by tradespeople such as electricians and plumbers.
  - some products may have limited demand and are produced for individual customers to meet their own specifications. These made-

to-measure products are produced using job production methods.
  - some markets are **niche markets**, where a small number of customers demand particular goods from a business, such as a jeweller selling expensive watches in a small town.
- **Capital** may be in short supply. The owners of small businesses will have limited savings, retained profits may be small and banks may be unwilling to lend money to such small businesses because of the risks involved in lending. When banks do lend, interest rates may be high.
- **Desire of the owner**. Some entrepreneurs are content with operating small businesses. They don't want the pressure or the complications of managing larger enterprises.

> **Niche markets** are those involving a small and well-defined segment of the population. All marketing efforts for a product are aimed at that market.

How are small businesses able to survive?

Large businesses have many advantages over those that operate on a small scale. They:
- charge lower prices
- have a greater range of goods
- can advertise more widely.

However, small businesses can compete by being different from their larger competitors.
- They provide their customers with **personal service**. The owner of the business usually works in the business, so is close to customers and may offer informal credit and delivery.
- **Knowing the customers** means the business owner is able to greet them in a friendly, welcoming manner. This helps encourage customers to return and maintains customer loyalty.

- The owner will be aware of individual **customer needs** and can provide goods and services to meet these needs.
- As part of this, the business may provide goods and services at **convenient times** for their customers, by opening for longer hours and during public holidays.
- The owner will work alongside their employees, so there is close **supervision of staff**. This helps ensure that workers are providing the appropriate personal service and attention required to meet the needs of customers.
- Small businesses are often found **in local communities**, so they are close enough for customers to buy products to meet their needs without having to travel to shopping centres or out of town sites.

Now test yourself

1 Why do small businesses find it difficult to raise capital?
2 Suggest three ways in which large businesses threaten the survival of small businesses.
3 Suggest two ways in which a small business can compete with larger businesses.
4 How important is it for small businesses to be geographically close to their customers?

Business location and site

Factors influencing where a business locates

The success of a business will often depend on where it is to be found. The wrong **location** will impact on suppliers and customers and on costs, prices and profits. Where the business will be located and, within that location, what is the best site, are two key considerations.

> **Location** is a geographical area where businesses may be found.
>
> **Site** is a specific place within a geographical area.

Location

When choosing the location, a business's owners will consider the following factors:

- How close they are to the **market**. Will there be plenty of customers near enough to buy goods? Will there be high costs in transporting the goods to consumers? If the goods are heavy and bulky they will need to produce goods close to the customers.
- How close they are to **raw materials**. Will there be high costs in transporting the materials to the factory? If the materials are heavy and bulky but the finished product is light, they will need to be close to the raw materials.
- Where will **costs** be at their lowest? Transport costs are important as are the costs of renting land and paying workers.
- What is the state of the **infrastructure**? That is: roads, rails, ports, the availability of power and also the availability and speed of broadband/internet.
- How close they are to the **labour supply**. This is not just about numbers but is also about the skills, qualifications and experience of the workers in an area.

Site

Once the entrepreneur has settled on the right location, a place (or '**site**') must be found within that location. Business owners will consider:

- The **accessibility** of the site is linked to the state of the infrastructure. Good roads will be needed to get workers and materials into the business and the finished product out. In the case of shops, business owners will want it to be accessible for their customers, so the closeness of railway stations, bus stops or car parks is important.
- For shops, **footfall** is also important. This is the number of people entering a shop or shopping area over a given time. The higher the footfall, the busier and more visible the business is likely to be.
- The **cost** of buying or renting the site will affect profits. Town centre sites are usually popular and, as such, expensive. Businesses not as reliant on lots of customers often choose cheaper out-of-town sites instead.
- The **size** of the site for present use and the possibilities for expansion will be a consideration.
- The **proximity** or **closeness** to competitors for bad or good reasons. Competitors may attract customers away from the business or they may lead to an increase in footfall, bringing more customers.
- **Personal reasons**, such as family considerations, may affect the site. For example, the owner may choose a site near to their family home.

Now test yourself

1. Which type of business will need to be located close to its source of raw materials?
2. What is meant by the term infrastructure?
3. Suggest three stakeholders who benefit from an accessible site.
4. The closeness to competitors can be good or bad for a business. Explain why.

TESTED

The interdependent nature of business

Role of the main functions in a business

In setting up and running a business, the entrepreneur needs to appreciate that the parts of a business do not operate alone. Most large businesses will be organised into departments that perform specific tasks or functions. Each department works to meet the aims and objectives of the business. Failure in one part can lead to failure of the entire enterprise. The areas of most businesses will include:

- **Business operations**. This involves the owners and managers making the most of all the assets owned by the business, to convert those assets into quality finished goods and services.
- **Marketing**. This area works to ensure that the right goods are in right place, at the right time, at the right price to make a profit. This will require the department to organise the advertising and promotion of the products.
- **Human resources** deal with the people needed to manage, produce and sell the goods to help the business to make a profit.
- **Production** involves combining the assets of the business to produce the goods and services that are to be sold.
- **Finance** pays for the assets and resources used to produce the goods and services and receives the payments for that output from customers.

> **Note**
>
> This topic is to be found in this part of the WJEC Specification but comes later in the Eduqas Specification.

> The **interdependent nature of business** means how the functions of a business are linked and how they affect each other.

These parts of the business cannot work independently of the other departments. They are interdependent. The table below shows examples of interdependence of business departments.

Business operations	Marketing	The department will need to know when the products will be ready so they can be available on the market after being promoted.
	Human resources	Workers will be recruited and trained to ensure the efficient operation of the department.
	Production	The raw materials will need to be available before production takes place and logistics will need to be organised to transport goods to the consumer.
	Finance	Raw materials will need to be sourced and costed. Suppliers of materials and providers of storage will need to be paid by this department. Costs will need to be monitored.
Marketing	Human resources	Workers will be recruited and trained to ensure the efficient operation of the department.
	Production	The department will need to know when the products will be ready, so they can be available on the market after being promoted.
	Finance	Advertising agencies and media will need to be paid. Promotion costs will need to be monitored to find how successful marketing has been.
Human resources	Production	Workers will need to be recruited and trained to ensure the efficient operation of the department. There may be links with trade unions during a dispute over production.
	Finance	Workers will be recruited and trained to ensure the efficient operation of the department. Wages will need to be calculated and paid.
Production	Finance	Cost will need to be examined and prices determined to ensure that profits can be made.

Now test yourself

1 Suggest two responsibilities of the marketing department.
2 Outline how human resources supports the other parts of the business.

Businesses do not operate in isolation. To survive and to earn profits, businesses need to be able to respond to events happening elsewhere.

Technological influence on business activity

Technology is important to business.
● It makes businesses more efficient to cut costs, increase sales and achieve greater profits.
● It is constantly changing: businesses need to respond to change.

Technology in the workplace

REVISED

Information technology (IT) packages are available to business to assist in:
● **administration** to write letters and keep records of transactions and accounts
● **communications** to inform stakeholders of the needs and the progress of business activity
● **recruitment** of workers by linking administration to communicate with possible recruits
● **stock control** to know which stocks are available and to co-operate with others to buy stock.

> **Tip**
>
> Knowledge of brand names or functions of packages is not required.

IT packages include:
● **word processing** for writing and storing information when communicating through letters and email, drafting agendas for meetings and writing reports
● **databases** for storing information about stock, customer contact details and staff records. Data can be searched when the information is needed
● **spreadsheets** for making calculations about costs, revenue and profits. Systems can create graphs and charts, as well as producing cash-flow forecasts and financial accounts
● **video conferencing and networking** is used for communication. Meetings can be held over great distances without participants having to leave their offices
● **presentational software** to help present information in a clear and dynamic way, either in meetings or online
● **computer graphic packages** to produce advertisements and promotional materials and to create newsletters
● **website design packages** to build websites in a similar way to the graphics packages.

Now test yourself

1 What is meant by the term information technology?
2 Suggest a package that a business may introduce to improve its administration when:
  (a) completing its financial records such as profit and loss accounts
  (b) finding a customer's telephone number
  (c) contacting a customer to remind him to pay an account
  (d) meeting managers at a distant branch.
3 Outline one way in which businesses benefit from developments in information technology.
4 Suggest a problem businesses face in introducing information technology.

TESTED

Technology in production

This mainly involves Computer Aided Design (CAD) and Computer Aided Manufacture (CAM).

CAD

Products are designed using computer software that can generate 3D images of the finished product. Details can be stored on computers and transferred online to others involved in the production process.

CAM

CAM has meant that machines are used in production but these are controlled by computers. There is therefore little human input into production: this is known as **automation**. Development in **robotics** is leading to machines looking like humans controlling machines.

> **Note**
>
> CAD and CAM are described here in the Eduqas Specification but are found in Production in the WJEC Specification.

> **Note**
>
> The terms automation and robotics are included in the WJEC Specification but not in the Eduqas Specification.

Benefits	Problems

● CAD uses computers to produce drawings of finished goods and parts: this speeds up design.
● Alternative designs can be considered.
● The appearance of goods can be seen before manufacture to find the most attractive design.
● There is no need to build models nor finished goods so money is saved.
● The computers used in design can easily transfer information to those used in production so measurements are transferred to the production process, resulting in fewer errors.
● CAM is ideal for use in flow production on a large scale.
● Standardised, more reliable products are manufactured leading to less waste during production.
● Fewer workers will be needed in the production process.
	● CAD and CAM are expensive to set up with:
	  – CAD requiring powerful computers and sophisticated software and
	  – CAM depending on costly robotics.
	● They require highly trained, well-paid engineers and technicians.
	● Training costs may be high.
	● The computer image may not provide a true image of the finished product, so models may still be needed.
	● There may be issues over worker redundancies when CAD and CAM are introduced.

Digital and social media communication with customers

The growth of computer, tablet and smartphone technology has changed the ways in which businesses are able to communicate.

Texts, messaging, emails and social media allow businesses to contact their customers immediately in response to queries, orders or complaints.

Social media was initially aimed at allowing individuals to communicate with each other, but businesses soon came to realise the potential of the new technology. It allows them to:
● market their goods through a different form of advertising
● interact with established customers and attract new ones
● respond to requests and complaints quickly
● follow trends in the market
● track the production and marketing strategies of competitors
● respond to publicity posted by other social network users.

Along with the positives, businesses also need to be aware that:
● costs may rise if expert technology workers need to be employed
● bad publicity will travel quickly across the market
● there may be fake publicity put out by some businesses
● cyber security can be an issue.

Many customers now use social media to review business products, services and customer care. They also compare products online and use this research to make more informed choices.

> **Tip**
>
> You should keep up to date with the latest types of communication technologies used by business.

> **Now test yourself**
>
> 1 Outline one advantage and one disadvantage for a business using CAM.
> 2 Outline two benefits for businesses using technology when communicating with customers.
>
> TESTED

The use of e-commerce and m-commerce technology

Goods can be purchased online via company websites, rather than in a physical shop. This is **e-commerce**. Purchases are paid for using debit or credit cards, and the goods are delivered either directly to a personal address, or to a retailer's store or collection point.

Developments in smartphone technology mean customers can now use also their mobile devices to purchase goods and services, regardless of where they are. This is **m-commerce**.

> **E-commerce** (or electronic commerce) is the act of buying or selling a product using an electronic system such as the internet.
>
> **M-commerce** (or mobile commerce) is the buying and selling of products through wireless handheld devices such as smartphones.

Evaluation of technology in selling

	Benefits	Problems

Business	• Not tied to expensive shopping sites.
	• Goods can be stored in warehouses on less expensive industrial estates.
	• Smaller businesses can enter the market more easily.
	• Customer service training is not needed, so less skilled and less expensive workers can be employed.
		• Potentially expensive set-up costs:
		  – website development
		  – warehouses updated for efficient despatch of goods
		  – stock control technology might need to be updated.
		• Goods need to be delivered to individual customers, rather than in bulk to retail outlets.
		• The return of unwanted goods needs to be organised and monitored.
		• Security measures must be introduced to protect against cyber-attacks.

Customer	• No need to travel to shops, saving time and money. • Goods are delivered to the customer's home. • Goods can be returned if they are not suitable. • The prices of goods have been lower.	• Goods that look good online may be not so good in real life. • Organising the return of unwanted goods can be inconvenient. • Unsuccessful deliveries need to be rescheduled. This problem has been reduced with retailers offering 'click and collect' enabling customers to purchase online but to collect the goods from retailer shops. • Trust can be an issue; customers are wary of fraud, shoddy goods or giving away personal details. • Contacting a business online or by telephone can be difficult. • Many businesses have closed their local shops and moved to online-only.

Evaluation of technology and business activity

Each use of technology has its own benefits and problems but businesses will adopt the new technologies if they help to reduce costs, increase output and increase sales. For stakeholders, the technology will affect such things as knowledge of products, the range of outlets and the security of jobs.

Now test yourself

1 What is meant by e-commerce?
2 Outline one difference between e-commerce and m-commerce.
3 How has the use of technology in selling goods helped businesses to cut their costs?
4 Outline two effects of the growth of e-commerce on business stakeholders.

Ethical influence on business activity

The conflict between business and ethics

When the owners of businesses make right and fair decisions for their stakeholders, they are being ethical. Government laws may force businesses to do what is morally right, but most firms have ethical policies to some degree, and many go beyond their legal requirements. The ethical needs of stakeholders differ.

Shareholders have invested their money in a business. They expect to receive a fair share of the profits. But dividends may be lower than what is fair as directors and managers award themselves high wages.

Employees: Providing well-trained workers with a good standard of living in the interest of the workers and their families is offered by ethical businesses. This leads to greater loyalty and productivity. However, paying low wages, in poor conditions, for long hours is a feature of some unethical businesses.

Customers earn businesses their revenue. Ethical businesses will:
- promote their goods so that customers are treated honestly and fairly
- provide goods and services in a quality appropriate to the price being paid
- not include harmful materials or ingredients in their products
- be aware of the concerns of consumers regarding treatment of animals.

Suppliers are treated ethically when:
- payments for supplies are made on time
- they are not forced to provide goods at lower prices than they can afford
- they sign contracts which are not ended at short notice by their customers.

Other ethical issues include:
- **Fair trade** products in which producers are not exploited by businesses and are paid a fair price so they can have a better quality of life.
- Businesses making sure that their suppliers treat their own stakeholders in an ethical manner.

Government can be treated unethically when businesses do not pay taxes.

Local communities are important to ethical businesses which:
- show consideration for the environment by reducing pollution
- provide facilities for communities such as improved roads, nurseries or libraries
- give charitable donations to local groups or sponsor local sports teams.

> **Business ethics** refers to whether a business decision is thought to be morally right or wrong. An ethical decision is made based on what is judged to be morally right.

Advantages and disadvantages of ethical policies

Benefits	Problems
• Many **customers are attracted** to products that are ethical, so sales are likely to increase. • Customers may be willing to pay higher prices for ethically sourced products. • **Employees** who are fairly treated may be **motivated** to work harder, particularly if they support the other ethical aims of the business. • **Suppliers** who are ethically treated will be **more stable** as they will, for example, be paid on time and will be more able to fulfil orders.	• Materials and labour will be more expensive when ethical policies are adopted. This will **increase costs** and if these cannot be absorbed by higher prices, **reduce profits**. • Ethical policies may be difficult to get approved by managers if there is a cost attached to them. • Lapses in the ethical image of the business may harm the business.

Now test yourself

1. What is meant by fair trade products?
2. Traidcraft sells goods produced by poor farmers. Why might it be an ethical business?
3. How are some businesses considered to be unethical in their dealings with governments?
4. Outline one reason why it is difficult for businesses to be ethical.

Environmental influence on business activity

The environmental costs of business activity

The environment is the natural world. It is:

- the wood, minerals and ores used to produce goods
- the places where goods and services are produced and sold
- the products such as oil and gas used by consumers.

But:

- The resources that are being used up are **finite** and cannot be re-created.

- The gathering of resources can **pollute** and destroy the homes of wildlife.
- The production of goods can **pollute** rivers, seas, land and air.
- Air pollution causes more carbon in the atmosphere, resulting in global warming and **climate change**.
- Increased waste, **congestion** and noise further spoil the environment.

What is sustainability and how can business respond to it?

Many businesses have **sustainability** as an objective. They can achieve this in a number of ways across different areas of a business:

- **Renewable energy** (such as wind or solar)
  - ○ Reduce reliance on energy produced using coal and gas.
- **Bio-degradable packaging**
  - ○ Use bio-degradable materials that are kinder to the environment.
- **Recycling schemes**
  - ○ Recycle materials to reduce the overall use of that material.
  - ○ Use recyclable materials for packaging.
- **Water efficiency**
  - ○ Reduce amount of water used and use it more efficiently.

- **Fair trade**
  - ○ Adopt fair trade products that rely on less intensive methods, which are less harmful to the environment.
- **Minimising waste**
  - ○ Use design and production techniques to ensure that fewer goods are discarded before they reach the consumer.
  - ○ Remove non-essential packaging of products.

> **Sustainability** refers to methods of production that can be continued in the long term without damage to the environment, or depletion of natural resources.

Environmentally friendly policies

Environmental policies will impact on businesses and their stakeholders.

Benefits	Problems

• Many customers are attracted to businesses that have environmental objectives.
• Customers buying environmentally ethical goods may be willing to pay higher prices for them.
• Some employees may have the same environmental values as their employers so will be motivated to work.
• Reduced wastage by environmentally friendly businesses may cut costs.
	• Business costs will rise
	  – as businesses seek environmentally friendly suppliers
	  – as modifications are made to production plants to reduce the effects of pollution
	  – as new products are developed to meet environmental needs.
	• Bad publicity for businesses that claim to be environmentally friendly but are found not to be so can lead to lower sales and lower profits.
	• Consumers will have to pay higher prices to pay for the extra costs of business.

> **Tip**
>
> Some of the benefits and problems of environmental policies are like those of ethical policies. The two can be considered together but read the question carefully to ensure that your answer relates to the correct policy.

Now test yourself

1. What is meant by the term sustainability?
2. Outline two problems businesses have when carrying out environmentally friendly policies.

Economic influence on business activity

Economic factors that affect business activity

The economic climate of a country changes over time. The economy is made up of all the stakeholders who interact with all the others to produce and consume goods and services. Changes in the decisions of one group of stakeholders can affect everyone. The following key economic factors can affect business activity: changing levels of consumer income, unemployment, inflation, interest rates and tax rates.

> **Note**
>
> There is no need to know economic theory relating to the economic influences on business activity.

Consumer income and unemployment

If unemployment is low, businesses must offer higher wages to attract new workers. With higher incomes, customers buy more goods and services, which can lead to businesses earning greater profits and, perhaps, growing. Note that when incomes rise, the amount spent on necessities is likely to remain the same but spending on luxury, or less essential, goods and services is likely to rise.

When unemployment is high, there are more people available for work and so wages do not need to be so high. Having less income available, customers spend less money, which can negatively impact business profits.

Low or falling unemployment will have similar effects on stakeholders as rising consumer incomes:

- **Shareholders** may receive higher dividends because of the higher profits (but falling unemployment may lead to higher labour costs).
- **Worker and manager** jobs will be more secure and wages will grow as businesses pay more to retain and attract workers from other businesses. Promotional opportunities may also increase as the business grows.
- The demand for some products will rise so prices paid by **customers** may increase.
- **Suppliers** may find an increased demand for their products so can charge higher prices. They may also find their costs will be rising (the labour required to meet the increased demand is more expensive).
- The **Government** should receive more from the taxes on income and, as the number of unemployed falls, the amount spent on benefits should fall. Money received from taxes on sales should also increase.
- The increased demand may lead to factory expansion, leading to increased environmental problems for **local communities**. Rising employment in business may also mean a fall in the number of workers available to work in the public sector.

> **Tip**
>
> Read any question carefully so your answer is about the required rise or fall in income.

When consumer incomes fall, and unemployment rises, their effects will be the opposite.

Now test yourself

1 Outline one effect of a fall in consumer incomes on each of (a) shareholders and (b) workers.
2 How do managers benefit from a rise in consumer incomes?
3 Consider one effect on local communities of a rise in the level of unemployment.
4 How do taxpayers benefit from a fall in unemployment?

Interest rates

When people borrow money, they pay a percentage of the amount each year to the lender: this is the interest rate. Lenders can set their own rates, but are guided by the rate set by the Bank of England.

A rise in the interest rate will mean it is more expensive for businesses to borrow money, so they may be less willing to borrow to invest in the business. Low interest rates should encourage businesses to borrow to invest in equipment. If the interest rate on a business loan increases, it will add costs to a businesses that they may not be able to afford. If this is the case, the business will be forced to close.

A rise in interest rates will affect stakeholders, for example:
- **Shareholders** are more likely to sell their shares as the interest on savings in a bank may give them a greater reward, so the value of shares may fall.
- **Customers** may be less willing to buy goods and services if the higher interest rates make it more attractive to save, rather than spend. Borrowing to buy goods will also become more expensive.
- If sales decrease (see **customers**), **workers and managers** may lose their jobs.
- Fewer sales and fewer workers means the **Government** may lose out on tax receipts. It will also pay more in benefits as unemployment rises.

Tax rates

There are two types of taxes: direct and indirect.

Direct taxes include:
- **Income tax**, which taxes people as a percentage of what they earn. This tax is also paid on the profits earned by the owners of sole traders and partnerships. The tax is paid at different rates so the higher the income, the greater the rate of tax.
- **Corporation tax**, which is a tax on the profits of companies.

Indirect tax is a tax on spending: the main such tax in the United Kingdom is **Value Added Tax (VAT)**. This is added to the cost of most goods and services, but not on some essential goods.

Changes in tax rates will affect the overall economy and particularly the costs, sales and revenue of businesses. A rise in tax rates will affect stakeholders, for example:
- **Shareholders** may find that the amount of money paid in dividends has fallen. They may move their money to areas that pay less tax.
- **Customers** may pay more income tax, so they will have less money to spend and prices may be higher if the rate of VAT rises.
- **Employees'** take-home incomes will be lower.
- The **Government** should earn greater tax revenue if workers continue to work and shoppers continue to buy.

> **Note**
>
> The differences between taxes are included in the Eduqas Specification but not in the WJEC Specification. The effects on stakeholders of changes in tax rates are required in both specifications.

> **Note**
>
> There is no need to have detailed knowledge of how the taxes are charged or of tax rates.

Now test yourself

TESTED ☐

1 Suggest two ways in which customers might be affected by a fall in interest rates.
2 Why might shareholders be concerned about a rise in interest rates?
3 Outline the difference between direct and indirect taxes.
4 How would workers benefit from a fall in taxes?

The Welsh economy and business activity

Note

This section is included in the WJEC Specification but not in the Eduqas Specification.

Wales has a population of about 3 million people of whom about 75 per cent are working age.

Most Welsh businesses are small- and medium-sized enterprises employing about 60 per cent of Welsh workers, and nearly half of these work in businesses with fewer than nine workers. The largest businesses are foreign-owned multinationals and others based in different parts of the United Kingdom. There is only one Welsh business in the top 100 British public limited companies.

In the past, there were more large Welsh businesses but these disappeared with the decline in mining and heavy industries. Wales still has manufacturing businesses involved in producing components for cars and aircraft. Other enterprises are found in leisure and tourism, customer services and in agriculture and forestry. Many employees work in the public sector in health and education.

Governments play a part in influencing business activity in Wales.

1 Central government in London is involved in the direction of the economy in the United Kingdom with control over tax rates, oversight of international trade and influence on interest rates.
2 Welsh Government in Cardiff deals with policies to do with economic and industrial development, tourism, the transport infrastructure, the environment and farming. Financial support and advice is also available to businesses and some taxes are also being devolved to Wales.
3 Local government. The local councils in Wales have their own economic development plans and schemes for helping businesses.

Unemployment rates are sometimes lower in Wales than in other parts of the United Kingdom but:
● Employment is generally in lower-paid jobs.
● The average age of the population is higher than that of the rest of the United Kingdom.

As a result:
● Consumers have less money to spend.
● Goods and services for the less well off must be provided by businesses.
● There are greater levels of poverty, which require support from governments including greater spending on health and social care.

Evaluation of business activity in Wales

Benefits	Problems
● Wage costs are lower than in other parts of the United Kingdom. ● Land prices are lower in Wales than elsewhere. ● Financial support and advice is available from the Welsh Government. ● Many businesses are attracted by the environment, which appeals to owners and employees. ● The universities have close ties with business to assist in the research and development of products.	● Wales is at the western edge of the United Kingdom so is not close to European markets despite the ports along the Bristol Channel in the south. ● The transport infrastructure is best travelling west to east by road and rail leading to much congestion. North to south routes are very limited. ● The physical geography of Wales also means that there are problems with the communications infrastructure for broadband and e-commerce.

Now test yourself

TESTED

1 How has the type of industry changed in Wales over the years?
2 Outline one reason why consumer incomes are lower in Wales than in the rest of the UK.
3 Outline two ways in which the Welsh Government can persuade firms to set up in Wales.
4 Suggest two factors that make it difficult for industry to grow in Wales.

The impact of globalisation on businesses

International trade

International trade happens when businesses buy or sell goods and services to or from other countries. Goods and services entering this country are **imports** and those leaving are **exports**. Trade takes place because:

- Not all goods, such as raw materials, are available in all countries.
- Certain goods and services can be produced more cheaply in some countries than in others.

Businesses in the United Kingdom usually import raw materials, food and capital goods. British businesses tend to export manufactured goods and services.

> **Exports** are goods and services that are produced in one country and sold in another one.
>
> **Imports** are goods and services that are bought from producers overseas.

Advantages and disadvantages of international trade to UK businesses

Benefits	Problems
<ul><li>It is part of the **growth** of the business. Businesses can expand elsewhere.</li><li>Businesses can enter **new markets** and gain:<ul><li>**increased sales**. Europe and the USA have long been markets for British businesses but growing economies in Asia and South America have increased the market for British producers</li><li>**increased profits** as sales increase</li><li>a **spreading of risks**. If sales fall in one area/country, British businesses can be protected by maintaining or increasing sales elsewhere.</li></ul></li><li>The **spreading of technical knowledge** means that British businesses can learn from foreign technical success, allowing them to improve UK products, or produce them more efficiently.</li></ul>	<ul><li>There may be **language barriers** so there may be problems in trading that may lead to higher costs, including.<ul><li>communication problems when marketing and selling</li><li>labelling of packaging</li><li>instruction manuals for technical exports.</li></ul></li><li>There may be **supply chain issues**. Distances are generally greater in international trade, so:<ul><li>transport costs will be higher</li><li>transport will take longer</li><li>appropriate forms of transport need to be found.</li></ul></li><li>There may be **foreign currency issues**. These might include:<ul><li>the costs of converting from pounds to foreign currencies</li><li>the different **rates of exchange** when buying and selling British pounds</li><li>changes in the rate of exchange between currencies. A rise in the value of the pound may benefit British exporters but if demand falls, revenues will fall. A fall in the value of the pound will make imported materials more expensive.</li></ul></li><li>Importing countries may impose **local taxes** or **tariffs** on goods to protect local producers.</li><li>There may be local **laws** and customs that will add to the costs of exporters. These may affect safety issues around electrical goods or environmental issues involving agricultural exports.</li></ul>

> A **supply chain** is the various processes involved in producing a product and distributing it to buyers.
>
> An **exchange rate** is the price of one currency expressed in terms of another.
>
> A **tariff** is a tax on an import. It is usually expressed as a percentage of the import's price.

Now test yourself

1 Why is international trade important in helping businesses to spread risk?
2 How do different legal systems affect the costs of British companies trading abroad?

What is meant by globalisation?

As international trade has grown, countries have become more interdependent with goods and services being required from sources around the world. Improvements in communication, technology and transport have helped to produce a global market for goods and services. **Globalisation** has led to:

- an **increase in international trade**: as consumer tastes have changed buyers have demanded goods and services from around the world
- the **development of multinational companies**
- **the free movement of labour** across international borders as some types of workers are in short supply and workers leave their own countries in search of greater opportunities and higher wages elsewhere
- **the free movement of capital** as businesses feel that they can set up anywhere in the world. Global businesses can make components in one country and assemble these into finished products in another.

> **Globalisation** is the trend for markets to become worldwide in scope.
>
> A **multinational company** produces goods and services in more than one country. They are also called transnational corporations.

Opportunities, threats and the impact of globalisation on UK businesses and stakeholders

The global economy has provided British businesses with a number of opportunities:

- To grow British businesses. This can lead to low costs resulting in:
  - greater profits so **shareholders** may receive higher dividends
  - the possibility of lower prices to the advantage of **customers**.
- Cheaper access to resources.
- Foreign business investment in Britain. The investments can provide:
  - more jobs for British **employees**
  - a greater variety of products for **consumers**
  - greater profits earned by these businesses providing higher tax receipts for the **Government** to spend on infrastructure projects.

The worldwide market is **very competitive**, however, and the greater efficiency of others in the global market can threaten the survival of British businesses in a number of ways:

- An increase in price competition, so:
  - Revenues may be reduced, leading to lower dividends for **shareholders**.
  - Businesses will aim for greater efficiency, so **employee** jobs will be at risk
  - **Suppliers** will be forced to receive less for their materials or lose sales to cheaper rivals.
- A larger firm may enter a new market through the takeover of a local business. This may:
  - threaten the jobs of local **employees**
  - threaten the sales of local **suppliers**.
- Global businesses can be very powerful, particularly in less developed countries. They can:
  - force lower wages on **employees**
  - ignore local laws on the environment and so impact on **local communities**
  - influence **Government** policies.

Now test yourself

1 What is meant by the term globalisation?
2 How do multinational companies take advantage of globalisation?
3 How might shareholders be affected by globalisation?
4 Outline two disadvantages workers might face because of globalisation.

TESTED

2 Influences on business

Multinational companies

Multinational companies are businesses with their headquarters in one country but which operate in other countries through their offices, factories and shops. Globalisation has resulted in many more multinational companies.

Should businesses become multinationals?

Benefits	Problems

• Multinationals establish a **global brand**. Most consumers know the names of multinational businesses. Sometimes the product is known by the name of the brand, such as Coke and Dyson. The brand name becomes a mark of the quality of products being produced by the multinational. This means that:
  – it is easier to compete on foreign markets against locally based businesses, so …
  – there are more customers in a wider market leading to greater profits, which …
  – encourage shareholders and others to invest.
• The global brand is recognised as a mark of quality, and one worth buying, so sales increase.
• As the businesses grow they can take advantage of **economies of scale** to minimise unit costs and to increase profits through:
  – bulk buying
  – improved technology
  – lower interest rates on loans.
• They can also gain from **increased market share**, which makes them more powerful in:
  – negotiating favourable deals with suppliers
  – determining the prices paid by customers.
• Multinationals can set up anywhere in the world to take advantage of **cheaper production costs**, such as:
  – lower wages paid to workers
  – cheaper rents for buildings and land
  – being close to raw materials or the producers of components to reduce transport costs.
• They can take advantage of changes in exchange rates of currencies to gain the greatest revenue at the lowest cost.
• Multinational companies can **avoid trade barriers** (such as tariffs) as these are not paid for goods produced in the countries in which they operate.
• Multinationals benefit from **government grants** to reduce the amount of money they need for investment. National governments are keen to attract businesses in order to reduce the levels of unemployment in their countries. This may also lead to lower taxes on business profits.
• Multinationals can take advantage of lenient employment laws around the world so they can pay lower wages perhaps in less favourable working conditions.
	• Multinationals are enormous businesses operating over great distances so:
	  – they are difficult to manage
	  – they may have communication problems
	  – they are expensive to run.
	• They must conform with the laws of the countries in which they operate. These may be different across the world in relation to consumer rights, planning, employment, product specifications and the environment.
	• Political systems may vary and, in some countries, there may be political unrest.
	• Exchange rate movements may act against multinationals leading to lower revenue and higher costs.
	• The aim of lower labour costs may lead to dis-satisfaction and lower morale among workers in the home country who may feel that their jobs have been exported abroad.

Now test yourself

1 Outline two effects of having a global brand.
2 Explain how multinational businesses can keep their costs down.
3 How do multinational businesses benefit from economies of scale?
4 Outline two problems faced by multinational businesses.

Tip

Do not confuse the advantages and disadvantages of being multinationals with those of trading abroad. Businesses can buy and sell goods abroad, but they are not multinationals.

Impact of multinationals setting up in the UK

Those responsible for government in the United Kingdom at local, regional and national levels are keen to attract foreign multinationals into their areas. This may have positive and negative impacts.

The **gig economy** refers to businesses that use mainly temporary workers who do not receive benefits such as guaranteed hours of work or holiday and sick pay.

De-skilling means that employees carry out tasks that are less complex and less numerous.

Benefits	Problems
Multinationals setting up new factories and offices need workers. **Jobs are created** so: ● more wealth is brought into the country ● more taxes are paid by the businesses and their workers ● less money is needed for unemployment benefits.	In some countries, the growth in the number of multinationals has led to the **exploitation of workers**. Employment laws in the UK have made this more difficult but it can still persist. For example, the **gig economy** – where workers are self-employed rather than employees of the business – means workers have fewer employee rights.
The increased output and sales lead to faster **economic growth** and an improved standard of living for all in the country.	Related to this is the **de-skilling** of workers. Many multinationals will produce components in different countries. UK factories will be used for assembling these using labour requiring few skills and less training.
There is **greater choice for consumers** who can chose goods from around the world.	The financial rewards will not be as great as those expected by the Government as: ● **profits do not stay in the UK**. Instead, they return to the home country of the business – which may also divert profits to other countries where tax rates are lowest. ● management positions are often taken up by nationals of the home country. The highest wages and salaries are reserved for these, so incomes for the production workers may not be high.
Multinationals may **introduce new technology** to an area or a country when they set up factories.	**Damage to the environment** can result if multinational companies have little interest in the impact their factories and workforce might have on the local environment.
To improve access to their factories and offices, multinationals will often contribute to infrastructure improvements.	Multinationals might move to this country for the lower wage or land costs or because of incentives provided by the Government. Such incentives may be expensive for taxpayers, and they may not produce the jobs expected.

Now test yourself

1 Outline the benefits a multinational setting up in an area will have for the unemployed in that area.
2 Suggest two ways in which multinationals create disadvantages for employees.
3 Suggest an advantage and a disadvantage of a multinational building a factory in an area.
4 Consider two problems that may result if the Government pays incentives to attract a multinational business.

The European Union

The European Union (EU) has a membership of 28 countries. In 2016 a majority of the electors of the UK voted to leave the EU.

The EU operates as a **single market**. This means:

- free movement of goods and services between member countries with no borders and customs duties for goods moved between such countries
- free movement of money around the EU
- free movement of people between member countries
- the same rate of tariffs being charged by members to goods being imported from non-member countries
- regulations affecting businesses are standardised across the EU:
  - ○ goods produced
  - ○ consumer protection
  - ○ employment laws
  - ○ environmental policies.

> **Tip**
>
> There is no need to have detailed knowledge of European Union organisations or institutions.

> The European **Single Market** made the EU one territory without any internal borders or regulations that could prevent the free movement of goods and services.

Evaluation of EU membership for businesses

Benefits	Problems
• The EU is the biggest market for British exporters with 400 million people. • Goods can be sent freely around the EU without paying duties and without being delayed at borders. • British companies are in competition with EU producers who must conform to similar laws. • Workers can be employed from across the EU. Problems over worker numbers or skills in the UK can be solved by finding workers from within the EU. • Money can be borrowed from across the EU to enable businesses to invest and grow.	• The free trade within the EU adds to the competition faced by British businesses. • Businesses are faced by regulations over the number and types of goods produced, the time worked by employees and the environment. • Complicated documents need to be completed to show that the rules are being kept. • It is more difficult for UK businesses to trade in markets outside the EU.

Evaluation of EU membership for other stakeholders

Stakeholder	Benefits	Problems
Customer	• Easy access to the products of 28 countries. • Prices will be lower because of the competition and because there are no tariffs on EU products. • Are protected by the rules covering the quality and safety of goods produced in the EU.	• Fewer goods may be available from countries that are not members of the EU. • Businesses will have to meet the standards of product set by the EU: this may lead to higher prices.

Employees	• Will be able to find work anywhere in the EU.
	• Non-EU businesses have set up in the UK to gain tariff-free access to the European market. These provide jobs for British workers.
		• More workers from around Europe can come to the UK. This may:
		  – reduce the number of jobs available for British workers
		  – reduce wage rates in Britain.

Government	• Can spend less on infrastructure projects as the EU will provide support to deprived areas in the UK.	• Must pay for membership of the EU. • Has reduced control over economic policies.

Now test yourself

1 How has membership of the European Union benefited British businesses?
2 Outline two consequences of membership of the European Union for British workers.

The impact of legislation on businesses

Businesses must operate within the rules and legislation of the country in which they operate. In order to protect stakeholders from unfair practices, the Government passes laws that aim to constrain businesses and make them responsible for their own business activity.

Employment laws

REVISED

Workers are protected from the unfair actions of employers with laws on the following:

- **Contracts of employment** must be given to employees within two months of starting work. Contracts cover pay, place of work, working hours, pensions and so on.
- **Discrimination**. Workers cannot be treated differently from other workers with regards to age, disability, gender, marital status, race, religion or sexual orientation.
- **Equal pay**. Different types of workers doing the same or similar jobs must be paid at the same rates. Employees have the right to a minimum wage, and the Government has set out the minimum hourly rates of pay workers must receive. This is known as the National Minimum Wage. You may also have heard of the National Living Wage. This is a significantly higher minimum level of pay that businesses can commit to, but it is not legally enforceable.
- **Unfair dismissal**. Workers cannot lose their jobs without good reason. Reasons include **redundancy** or lack of skill or misconduct by the worker. Workers cannot be dismissed because they are not liked by the employer, or they belong to a trade union, or they become pregnant, or they take their parental rights.
- **Safe working conditions (Health and Safety)**. Workers are entitled to be safe at work so injury or threats to their health are minimised.

The laws allow legal actions to be taken when workers have been treated unfairly.

A **contract of employment** is a legal document stating the hours, rates of pay, duties and other conditions under which a person is employed.

Discrimination is treating one person differently from another without having good reasons to do so.

Dismissal takes place when an employer ends an employee's contract of employment with the business.

Redundancy occurs when an employee is dismissed because a job no longer exists.

Consumer law

REVISED

Customers are protected from the actions of businesses when they buy goods and services with laws on the following:

- **Product quality**. Customers must be certain that the goods they buy are not damaged at the point of sale, are **fit for purpose** and as described. The laws show what the customer can do if goods do not meet these standards in terms of refunds, replacements or repairs. E- and m-commerce have resulted in additional laws around online selling.
- **Advertising**. Advertisements must be legal, truthful and honest, so goods and services offered for sale must be accurately described.
- **Trade descriptions**. Goods and services must be accurately described at the point of sale and on labels including the ingredients, use by dates and weights of products.
- **Safety of products**. These laws protect customers from being harmed by the goods they buy, such as in the materials used in manufacture or the cleanliness in preparing food.

Fit for purpose means that the goods do what they are supposed to do.

The laws allow legal actions if buyers have been treated unfairly.

Intellectual property law

Original works and processes created by businesses, inventors, writers, composers, performers and artists are protected from the unfair actions of other businesses and individuals. They can do this by using:

- **Patents**. Inventors can register their designs, which cannot be used by others without permission for up to twenty years after registration.
- **Copyright**. This prevents others using artistic works without permission. Such work includes books, music, film, paintings and computer programs.
- **Trademarks**. This protects brands and symbols from being used by others without permission. Businesses spend large sums of money to protect their brands.

The laws allow legal actions if **intellectual property** is copied.

> **Intellectual property** is inventions, works of art and books, as well as names, symbols and images used by businesses.

Now test yourself

1 What can a worker insist on within two months of starting a job?
2 Why is it difficult for an employer to dismiss a worker?
3 Why are there laws to protect customers from the suppliers of goods?
4 How can business be protected from others stealing their product designs?

The impact of legislation on businesses and their stakeholders

Employment, consumer and intellectual property laws can affect different areas of a business in different ways:

Costs and profits

Benefits	Problems
• Workers may be motivated to work harder and to increase their productivity. (Employment) • Consumers are more likely to buy goods if they can trust brands for quality, so prices of such goods may be higher, leading to greater profits. (Consumer)	• Costs may increase as: – higher wages are paid to workers (Employment) – quality checks are needed to ensure that goods are fit for purpose (Consumer) – output may be wasted where this does not happen (Consumer) – it may be expensive to create and protect intellectual property rights. (Intellectual)

Marketing and sales

Benefits	Problems
• Competitors are less likely to make false claims about products. (Consumer) • Brands and trademarks are protected so competitors are less likely copy these. (Intellectual)	• All goods and services must meet the standards advertised of quality and labelling or goods may need to be recalled to correct issues leading to (Consumer) ... • bad reputation across the product range of a brand. (Consumer)

Production

Benefit	Problem

● Consumers are more likely to buy the products of businesses if they have confidence in:
  – the quality and safety of the goods and services on offer and (Consumer)
  – the treatment of workers producing those products. (Consumer)
	● Businesses need to ensure that production methods comply with legislation to protect the wellbeing of employees and of consumers. (Employment and Consumer)

Human resources

Benefit	Problem
● Well-paid employees, working in a safe environment, are more likely to remain with businesses. The turnover of workers is reduced so recruitment and training costs are kept to a minimum. (Employment)	● It becomes more difficult to discipline and dismiss bad workers. Complicated and expensive legal processes must be followed. (Employment)

The stakeholders

Different stakeholders are also affected in different ways:

Benefits	Problems
● Prices can be increased so profits will rise and **shareholder** rewards will increase. ● **Employees** will receive higher wages and an improved standard of living. ● They will also be working in a clean, safe environment. ● There is less chance that **customers** will receive bad quality products or be deceived by dishonest advertising. They will have greater confidence in the brands they buy. ● This will extend into the weights and safety of food products. ● The **Government** will gain from the sale of protected foods with a healthier population and ● from the safe working conditions and more motivated workers. Workers are more likely to remain in their jobs so less money needs to be spent on benefits.	● Costs may be higher, so profits may be lower, as will be dividends to **shareholders**. ● **Customers** will have to pay higher prices to cover some of the costs of higher wages, payments for consumer protection and costs of maintaining intellectual property rights. ● Local and national **government** will need to monitor, control and enforce the legislation: this may be expensive.

Now test yourself

TESTED

1 Outline two ways in which laws may affect the costs of businesses.
2 Suggest two ways in which laws to protect consumers affect businesses.
3 How do intellectual property laws encourage publishing companies to produce books?
4 Outline one benefit and one problem to customers of consumer protection laws.

3 Business operations

Production

Methods of production

REVISED ✓

The purpose of business is to combine resources and to convert these into goods and services that are sold to make a profit. The first task is to create the product and this can be done by one of the following methods of **production**:

- Job production
- Batch production
- Flow (mass) production

> **Production** is the process of changing inputs such as labour into goods and services that can be sold.
>
> **Job production** is a method of production in which a product is supplied to meet the exact requirements of a customer.

Job production

In **job production** goods are produced to meet the exact needs of customers; they are made to order and are individually produced.

Evaluation of job production for the producer

Benefits	Problems
● The business may be able to charge higher prices because the goods are unique and so ● earn greater profits. ● Workers will be highly motivated as the work varies, and they have the satisfaction of seeing goods produced from beginning to end. A more content workforce can lead to lower worker turnover. ● The business will have greater personal links with customers to meet their personal needs. The producer may be in touch with the customer from the design stage and during production.	● As each product is different, the production process is more expensive for each good produced. Materials may have to be purchased in smaller quantities. ● If higher prices cannot be charged it may be difficult to make a profit. ● Skilled workers will be required. These may be difficult to recruit and will be paid higher wages. ● The work is labour intensive, so there are fewer opportunities to introduce technology into the process. ● When technology can be introduced, it will be expensive and may be underused. ● The business may need to change the tools required for each new type of good being produced.

Evaluation of job production for the stakeholders

Benefits	Problems
● As they are highly skilled, workers will be paid higher wages. ● Workers have the satisfaction of seeing the goods produced from beginning to end. ● Customers will be supplied with unique products, which they may have had some input in designing. ● The skills of the workers and the time taken to produce will mean products are of a high quality.	● Worker skills may not be transferable into other areas so it may be more difficult for them to find jobs elsewhere if demand falls. ● Customers will have to pay higher prices because of the high cost of production. ● Customers will need to wait for delivery of their individually produced goods.

Now test yourself

TESTED ✓

1 What is job production?
2 How do workers benefit from job production?

Batch production

Batch production involves making a fixed quantity of goods before switching to another type of good. It is suited to producing identical goods that are not demanded in large quantities.

> **Batch production** occurs when groups of items move together through different stages of the production process.

Evaluation of batch production for the producer

Benefits	Problems

● More goods are produced than for job production so:
  – Producers will benefit from economies of scale.
  – Producers will be able to sell more goods.
● Machinery can be used in producing different goods.
● Workers can be employed and trained to perform set tasks.
	● Where the resetting of machinery is difficult, time and money is used between the production of batches.
	● Materials and finished products will need to be stored: this will be expensive.

Evaluation of batch production for the stakeholders

Benefits	Problems
● Prices are generally lower than for goods produced using job production. ● Consumers have a range of products to choose from.	● Goods lack the individuality found in those produced using job production. ● Workers can be demotivated in performing the same tasks every day.

Flow production

Also known as mass production, **flow production** involves partly finished goods moving along an assembly line with parts added through the process. All goods are the same and are produced in large quantities.

> **Flow production** occurs when an item moves continuously from one stage of the process to another, in large-scale production of identical items.

Evaluation of flow production for the producer

Benefits	Problems
● Workers can be employed and trained quickly to perform set tasks. ● Businesses can produce enormous quantities of goods. ● This enables them to gain from economies of scale so ● each good can be produced at the lowest possible cost.	● Factories are expensive to set up and run as production sites will be large and machinery is costly. ● Production can be inflexible as sites are so large and workers are trained in specific skills so it is difficult for businesses to respond quickly and cheaply to changes in consumer demand. ● Labour issues found in the monotony of day-to-day work may lead to absenteeism, high levels of worker turnover and lower quality workmanship. ● Large quantities of stock may need to be stored. ● Breakdowns in one part of the flow can cause bottlenecks and delays in other parts.

Evaluation of flow production for the stakeholders

Benefits	Problems
● Mass produced goods are generally cheaper than those produced using other methods. ● Consumers can choose from a wide range of products to be able to enjoy higher standards of living.	● There is less consumer choice regarding design or colour. ● Workers can be demotivated in performing the same tasks every day.

Now test yourself

TESTED ✓

1 What is meant by the term batch production?
2 What is meant by the term mass production?

Quality

What is quality?

Consumers have their own standards as to what they mean by **quality**.
- When buying goods, customers expect that the product should do the job that it was intended to do, and that it lasts for a long time.
- When buying services, the expectation is that a good job has been done.

> **Quality** involves meeting a standard for a good or service in order to meet consumer needs and expectations.

How do businesses achieve quality?

- Buying quality **raw materials and parts**.
  - Poor quality components are more likely to lead to poor quality products.
  - Poor quality materials may do harm to customers.
- Having the best **production processes** and equipment to provide services bearing in mind the type of good or service being produced.
- **Employing the right quality of workers**, with the right skills and experience. **Training** may be available for all employees to ensure that they update and improve their skills.
- Using **quality assurance** strategies. These ensure that quality is built into the production process. All relevant stakeholders are expected to maintain quality in their input into the production of goods and services.
- Using **quality control** during and at the end of the production process to make sure that goods meet the required standards.
- **Interacting** with customers:
  - by asking for feedback after goods and services have been provided
  - by dealing with complaints adequately and quickly.

> **Quality assurance** is a guarantee given by producers to consumers that certain standards have been met throughout the production process.
>
> **Quality control** involves inspecting a sample of goods produced at the end of the production process to ensure that specifications have been met.

Why is quality important to a business?

Benefits	Problems

- **Satisfying customer expectations**. Customers know that the type and quality of goods and service from a fast food takeaway will be different from that at a plush restaurant.
- It **increases customer satisfaction** so that when customers enjoy the quality of a product they are more likely to return to buy the product or other goods produced by the same manufacturer.
- It helps to **increase sales** with return customers and with sales to others who have heard product recommendations.
- It **reduces costs** as:
  – well-designed goods do not need to have costly modifications
  – faulty goods do not need to be recalled or replaced.
- It **reduces waste**.
- It sometimes allows businesses to charge higher prices as customers will be more willing to pay more for products recognised for their quality.
	- Quality assurance can be expensive as:
	  – suppliers will expect to be paid higher prices for their quality checks
	  – labour will need to be trained.
	- Quality control can be expensive as supervisors will need to be employed to monitor and sample production.
	- The growth of businesses with more suppliers and larger scale production can make it more difficult to manage quality.

Now test yourself

1 What is meant by the term quality?
2 Outline the difference between quality control and quality assurance.
3 Describe three ways in which businesses gain from producing quality products.
4 Why might the production of quality products be costly for businesses?

The supply chain

Every business needs resources to be able to produce goods and services. Items such as stationery for the office and food for the canteen will also be required. Care must also be taken in knowing where the suppliers obtained their materials and how the finished product reaches its destination. This is the **supply chain**.

> A **supply chain** is the various processes involved in producing a product and distributing it to buyers. Managing the supply chain includes procurement of supplies, logistics and stock control.

Procurement

The first task in **procurement** is to find suppliers: this is **sourcing**. Businesses must identify suitable suppliers in order to purchase the supplies they need. To do this they will send enquiries to businesses and carry out further research regarding:

- the prices of goods being supplied and details about discounts for bulk purchases. These will impact on the prices charged and the profits earned by the producer.
- details about the resources that can be supplied such as:
  - their quality – complaints about the quality of finished products might damage a business's reputation and add to the costs of the manufacturer
  - the range of products that can be supplied – it may suit a business to obtain a variety of resources from the same supplier.
- information about the supplier such as:
  - its reputation
  - its reliability in terms of the quality of goods produced and delivery
  - its payment terms such as the time allowed to pay for supplies and any discounts for prompt payment
  - its ethical and environmental policies and reputation.
- details about delivery such as:
  - its cost
  - the speed of delivery. The distance between the business and its supplier may be an issue. Businesses do not want to delay production because supplies of resources have been delayed.
  - the ability to deliver at short notice or within certain times.

> **Procurement** will involve selecting suppliers, establishing the terms of payment and negotiating the contract.
>
> **Logistics** refers to the movement of goods, services, information and money throughout the production process.

Logistics

Once a supplier of materials has been found, the purchase and movement of supplies must be managed so that they are transported to the manufacturer, processed and distributed to the consumer. All this is the concern of **logistics**, which aims to get the right goods, to the right place, at the best price and in the right condition. The stages in logistics include:

- the buyer selecting and paying for the materials or goods
- agreeing a delivery date
- organising transportation. This may be by road, rail, sea or air perhaps depending on:
  - how quickly the goods are needed
  - the distance they are to be transported
  - the cost of transport in relation to the value of the goods
  - the nature of the goods: are they fragile or bulky or valuable?
- organising the storage – or warehousing – of goods so that they can be kept securely in good condition
- distributing the goods, either to the next stage (possibly involving wholesalers and retailers) or directly on to the end user (the final consumer).

Now test yourself

1. Where does the supply chain begin and when does it end?
2. Why is sourcing important in the procurement process?
3. When sourcing goods, why is it necessary to have full details about the suppliers?
4. How are procurement and logistics closely linked?

TESTED

Stock control

Stock forms an important part of the supply chain. Stock can include:
- the materials needed to produce goods
- partly finished goods within the production process
- finished goods awaiting sale to customers.

Stock levels that are too low or too high can cause problems for businesses.

There are two main systems of stock control:

1 The **traditional method** (or '**just in case**') involves businesses warehousing stock they known they might need. As goods are produced, or sold, stock levels are run down until new stock is ordered.

2 **Just in time (JIT)** involves stock being delivered when it is required. Suppliers will deliver the correct goods or materials, in perfect condition, to the appropriate part of the factory at a certain time.

Both methods of stock control have positive and negative aspects.

> **Note**
>
> The construction and interpretation of stock control diagrams are **not** required.

> **Just-in-case** production holds stocks just in case there is a delay from suppliers or a sudden unexpected increase in demand.
>
> **Just-in-time** production holds as little stock as possible. Items are ordered just in time to be used.

Evaluation of traditional stock control (just in case)

Benefits	Problems

• Stock is available nearby, so production will not be held up by delivery delays.
• Bulk purchases of stock mean larger discounts, so costs are lower.
• The quality of stock can be checked as delivery is made.
• Stock can be kept in the correct environment.
	• It is expensive to store materials and finished products in warehouses.
	• Stocks are moved from the warehouse to the factory. This makes damage to materials more likely.
	• Stock and materials may lose their value as:
	  – they deteriorate (if stored in the wrong environment)
	  – they become out of date (as new materials and processes are developed)
	  – a downturn in business means materials are not needed, but they cannot be resold at the price that was paid for them.

Evaluation of just in time

Benefits	Problems
• Stock is bought when it is needed and goods are sold when they are demanded, so warehouses are not needed. • Materials are likely to be in good condition as they are brought directly from the manufacturer. • Up-to-date materials can be bought. • There is little waste as the business is only buying what it needs. • Stock is delivered to where it is needed, so there is less chance of damage.	• If suppliers run out of materials, production may have to stop. • There may be delays in deliveries because of the weather or traffic conditions. • Deliveries will be in smaller quantities, so there will be lower discounts than for bulk purchases.

Computerised stock control

Businesses need to know how much stock they have and where it is and computerisation has greatly helped with this. As stock arrives, bar codes can be read automatically and the amount is added to the total. Conveyor belts, controlled by computers, carry the stock to be stored. When it is taken from store, bar codes are used to show this and computers order new stock. The information is available throughout the business.

> **Now test yourself**
>
> 1 Outline two ways in which stock is important to businesses.
> 2 Suggest two benefits of traditional stock control.
> 3 Why have many businesses adopted just in time in their production process?
> 4 How has computerised stock control helped in stock control?
>
> TESTED

Business departments and the supply chain

The supply chain works in relationship with different business departments in order for the business to achieve its overall aims and objectives.

- The **Operations** Department is responsible for procurement and logistics in the supply chain for the business, but other departments will be involved in the process.
- **Finance**. Goods must be bought at the best possible price and bills must be passed on to Finance to be paid.
- **Marketing** will encourage the purchase of goods by the customers. The greater the quantity demanded, the more resources move along the supply chain and to customers.
- The **Sales** Department will organise the distribution of goods to wholesalers and retailers for sale to the final consumer. Failures in the supply chain will mean that orders will not be met.
- **Human Resources** will ensure that workers are available to accept materials into the business, deal with stock in the warehouses and help distribute goods to the next stage in the supply chain.

> **Note**
>
> For more detail on these departments see the section on Human Resources.

Stakeholders and the supply chain

Supply and logistical decisions can impact positively and negatively on a business and its stakeholders. Some of the individual stakeholder's decisions are detailed as follows:

- **Managers** within these individual departments will need to make decisions on sourcing supplies. Specifically, should supplies be purchased locally, nationally or globally? Should there be considerations about buying from less developed countries? The answers will be based on:
  - the **quality** and **cost** of the materials. There needs to be a balance between the two. Cheaper resources can lead to inferior goods being produced, which may impact on the reputation of the business.
  - the **logistics** of moving materials to the factories and distributing the finished goods to the consumer.
  - **warehousing** This is important in regards to how goods are stored but, to reduce costs and to have goods available when demanded, measures are also needed to control the amount of stock.
- **Shareholders** will want costs to be minimised but the quality of products to be maintained to ensure sales at as high a price as possible to earn high profits.
- **Employees** will be concerned about how changes in the supply chain and the production process will impact on jobs, wages and working conditions.
- **Customers** expect to reliably receive the best quality products at the most appropriate prices. Changes in the supply chain can impact on price and quality, affecting customer satisfaction.
- **Suppliers** will want to ensure that they continue to supply their customers so they need to maintain the quality of their materials and the efficiency and reliability of their logistics. Failure to do so could result in the work being given to other suppliers.
- The **Government** passes laws to ensure the fairness of the supply chain and to provide the basis of the infrastructure to allow the supply chain to operate efficiently.
- **Local communities** will be affected by supply chain decisions because these may affect the environment particularly if production processes are changed, but they may benefit from any jobs created with changes to the supply chain.

> **Now test yourself**
>
> 1 Suggest two functions of the Finance Department in the supply chain.
> 2 How will delays in the supply chain affect the Sales Department of a business?
> 3 How might a decision by a business to change its supplier affect customers of that business?
> 4 Why are the suppliers to a business concerned about providing the right goods on time?
>
> TESTED ✓

Sales process

From a business point of view, the final link in the supply chain is when goods or services are sold to customers. This is where revenues are earned and profits made. To ensure sales are maximised, businesses need to follow a **sales process**.

Stages in the sales process

- Employees must have a thorough knowledge of the product being sold. This helps to inform customers of the features and benefits of the product or service. At this stage, the seller should show confidence in the product.
- Understand the needs and wants of customers. This may be done by:
  - on a wide scale, carrying out market research to find the level of customer demand for the product
  - asking questions when the customer enquiries about products
  - using loyalty cards and itemised receipts at the point of sale to show what the customer has bought as an indicator of future sales opportunities.
- Responding to questions to identify sales opportunities.
- Informing customers of the features and benefits of the product or service.
- Closing the sale so that the customer agrees to buy the good or service.
- Following up on the sale by asking whether the customer is pleased with the good or service or how they could have been better served.
- Offering **after sales service** such as delivery or maintenance or repair facilities for technical goods.

> **Sales process** involves a series of steps taken from when the potential buyer meets the prospective seller until after the final sale is made.
>
> **After sales service** is the meeting of customers' needs after they have purchased a product – for example, by repairing or servicing the product.
>
> **Customer engagement** occurs when the business and customers communicate throughout the sales process.

Evaluation of the sales process

An efficient sales process acts to the advantage of stakeholders in the business.

Benefits	Problems
<ul><li>The **shareholders** will find greater profits as sales and revenues will be maintained because of consumer satisfaction in the products and the sales process. Errors in the process will have the opposite effect.</li><li>**Employees** will have greater confidence in selling goods with their increased knowledge gained from appropriate training.</li><li>**Customers** will be more likely to have confidence in the products bought from knowledgeable sales staff.</li></ul>	<ul><li>Training of employees can be expensive perhaps leading to …</li><li>higher prices paid by customers.</li></ul>

Customer engagement

This usually means face-to-face verbal communication between employee and customer. Much of this area is covered above but in summary, **customer engagement** involves:

- understanding needs and wants of customers with the sales staff asking what the customer requires
- informing customers of the features and benefits of the product or service so that the customer can choose to buy or not
- closing the sale after the customer has agreed to buy and the means of payment has been agreed
- following up as the seller asks about the quality of service
- after sales with:
  - arrangements for delivery and installation of heavy or technical goods
  - dealing with complaints.

> **Note**
>
> The term **customer engagement** is used in the WJEC Specification but not in the Eduqas Specification.

Now test yourself

1 Why should employees have a good knowledge of the products they sell?
2 When does the closing of the sale take place?

The sales process in different situations

REVISED ✓

Retail sales

This involves the use of shops where customers can view the goods, make comparisons, check goods for size and quality and so on.

Evaluation of retail sales

For customers and businesses, retail sales have a number of potential benefits and disadvantages:

	Benefits	Problems
Customer	• Comparisons can be made between goods and retailers. • Information can be requested, and advice given, from the seller, due to their product knowledge. • Terms can be discussed with the seller. • Goods can be received on payment.	• Prices may be higher than for online sales. • Customers will need to travel to purchase goods. • Buyer may be influenced by the salesmanship of the seller and may impulse buy.

Business	• There will be closer links with the customer so:
	  – the seller will be in touch with consumer wants
	  – there is greater opportunity to persuade the customer to buy.
	• The business can locate themselves where customers are more likely to be found.
		• Expensive premises will be required.
		• There may be greater competition for customers in city centre sites.

Online sales

Many businesses have set up websites to display and promote their goods and services. Large-scale retailers often combine their retail and online sales to attract customers from different areas. Developments in e- and m-commerce have helped in the sales process. Small-scale businesses have been able to take advantage of selling online with their own websites or through third party businesses such as Amazon and eBay.

> **Tip**
>
> The advantages and disadvantages of e- and m-commerce to customers and businesses were considered earlier.

High value sales

Businesses know that every customer deserves their best level of service, but high-value customers are vital to its success. These wealthy customers are more likely to make a purchase from the business, and have the ability to influence the behaviour and opinions of other potential high-value customers. To increase high-value sales and customers businesses can:

- build long-term relationships with customers by employing sales staff who are honest, knowledgeable and caring
- create brand loyalty by providing high quality goods and exceptional service so the customer will want to return
- upsell and cross-sell. The former means that the customer is persuaded to buy higher priced alternatives and the latter that the customer will buy additional goods
- choose the right rewards and incentives, with loyalty cards and other incentives for regular customers
- use a variety of ways for the business to stay in touch with its customers, whether by face-to-face conversations, telephone, email or social media
- help customers tell others about their experience of the business. Social media and travel websites allow customers to tell others about the quality of products purchased.

> **Now test yourself**
>
> 1 Outline two ways in which the customer benefits from shopping in store.
> 2 Suggest two disadvantages for businesses selling goods in shops.
> 3 How have small businesses benefited from e-commerce?
> 4 Outline why high-value customers are important to a business.
>
> TESTED ✓

The relationship between sales and other functions in the business

The sales process relies on the relationship between departments.

- **Finance**. The Finance Department must keep records of the income from sales and the costs and analyse these to ensure that profits are earned.
- **Marketing** will help to identify the needs of the customers, and ensure that staff have sufficient knowledge to sell goods and services.
- **Production** will aim to manufacture the goods to the highest standard so that customers are not disappointed with the goods bought.
- **Human Resources** will ensure that workers are available to sell the goods and that they have the training, the knowledge and the skills to sell products effectively.
- **The supply chain**. The goods will need to be supplied to the customer in the right condition, at the right place and at the right time.

The importance of good customer service and meeting customer expectations

Customers expect good **customer service**. They see this in:

- the employees with:
  - their appearance, so workers are clean, tidy and approachable
  - the extent of their knowledge, to be able to answer customer questions accurately
  - their communication skills, so workers are polite and friendly, listen to customer requests and respond clearly to avoid misunderstandings
- the business with:
  - the state of the sales **premises** around cleanliness, signage and the availability of toilets
  - the payment methods available
  - the after sales service regarding delivery and maintenance
  - the extent of training given to staff
- the products with:
  - quality, in relation to the price of the products
  - appropriate information and display at the point of sale
  - services being reliable so that the business does the work on time
  - regards to safety around mechanical and electrical goods, and also transport services.

When customer expectations are met, this will lead to:

- **increased customer loyalty** as they are more likely to return to purchase products
- **increased customer spending** when they return and are more likely to buy a range of goods and services offered by the business
- **improved reputation**, so
- **new customers are attracted**, so
- businesses may be able to charge more for its products
- the increased sales and revenue can lead to greater profits
- customers being attracted away from competitors to increase the market share of the business.

> **Customer service** is the part of a business's activities that is concerned with meeting customers' needs as fully as possible.
>
> **Premises** are the buildings used by businesses: these may include offices, shops and factories.
>
> **Customer loyalty** means that a business's customers make repeat purchases because they prefer the business's products to those of its rivals.

Now test yourself

1 List three features of service customers expect.
2 Suggest two reasons why customer loyalty is important to a business.

When businesses and customers interact

Interactions between businesses and customers take place:
- when customers want to know of product availability and features
- at the point of sale of the goods and services as the products are paid for
- if there are complaints or queries about quality or delivery of goods
- if after sales services are available.

Features of good customer service

In retail sales, the premises and the staff are the first contact the customer has with the business. In telephone sales, the customer speaks to an employee. These contacts are an important part of good customer service. Customer service involves:
- **greeting the customer** so the customer feels welcomed and at ease with the business. This might involve a simple 'Good morning'.
- **interacting with the customer** with polite conversation before asking how the customer can be helped.
- **identifying customer needs and wants** by being specific about the products that the customer wants.
- **encouraging feedback** from the customer to find the reaction of the customer to the service. This may involve feedback forms or postings on social media.
- **responding to feedback** to show how the business responds to praise or otherwise following the purchase of goods and services.

> **Feedback** is the response by a customer following the purchase of a good or service. This will be used by the producer to improve what has been produced.

Online customer service

Online businesses have fewer personal links between themselves and their customers, but still need to provide good quality service to maintain sales. They do this by adapting the traditional features of good customer service for the online world.
- **Greeting the customer.** The customer needs to feel welcomed onto the website with a clear and easy to navigate homepage and site.
- **Interacting with the customer.** Online technology means that businesses have a record of previous purchases by the customer. This allows them to directly offer these (or similar) items to the customer.
- **Identifying customer needs and wants** means being specific about the goods or services that are being sought by the customer.
  - Images, videos and descriptions of products that are available can help the customer decide what to buy.
  - It should be easy for the customer to place an order, make payment, and organise a delivery.
- **Encouraging feedback.** This may be:
  - presale with
    - a 'Frequently Answered Questions' section of the website, which shows what previous customers wanted to know of the product
    - contact details, so that customers can ask their own questions
  - post-sale, encouraging email or social media feedback.
- **Responding to feedback** to show that the business responds to (and cares about) comments regarding its goods and services. This can be done either on its own website, or on social media.

Now test yourself

1. Why is the right greeting of customers helping a business to reach its aims and objectives?
2. How can an employee make a customer feel confident in the service provided by a business?
3. Why should a business respond to feedback from its customers?
4. Outline two differences between customer service in shops and that online.

TESTED

4 Finance

Sources of finance

Finance is the money needed to start and run a business. When starting, money may be needed for buildings, equipment, vehicles and advertising. Later, finance will be used for growth and to improve efficiency.

Internal and external sources of finance

REVISED

Finance is available from **internal sources** and **external sources**.

Internal sources

Owner's capital

This is money put into the business by the owner from personal savings.

> An **internal source** of finance is money that is available from within the business.
>
> An **external source** of finance refers to money that comes from outside the business.

Benefits	Problems
• The money is available without needing to go through complicated application processes. • No **interest** is charged on the money. • Money does not have to be repaid. • The owner keeps control of the business. • Issues around unlimited liability do not exist.	• The money will not be available to spend on other needs. • Interest will be lost when the money is withdrawn from savings accounts. • The owners may not have sufficient funds saved.

Retained profit

When any business earns profits, the owners or directors can decide to spend these on themselves or to distribute them to shareholders, or they can keep the profits and invest them in the business immediately, or in the future. These are **retained profits** or ploughed back profits.

The benefits and problems associated with retained profit are the same as those found for owner's capital. One additional problem is that there may be some conflict between the shareholders in a limited company and the directors on the level of dividends compared with the amount of money retained for future use.

Selling assets

Some businesses will have possessions that they no longer need. These assets can be sold off in order to raise finance. Such possessions can include outdated or damaged stock, outdated machinery and unused land and buildings. If a business decides to concentrate on producing a smaller range of goods, they may also sell off any unwanted parts of the business.

> **Interest** is a payment made in order to borrow money. It means a business pays back more than it borrows.

> ### Now test yourself
>
> 1 Explain one disadvantage of using personal savings as a source of finance for a sole trader.
> 2 What is meant by the term ploughed back profits?
>
> TESTED

Benefits	Problems
• No interest is charged. • The owner keeps control of the business. • Issues around unlimited liability do not exist. • The business will no longer have to pay storage, security or maintenance costs for assets no longer required.	• It will take time to find buyers for the assets. • The assets might have cost more than will be received from selling to others. • The sale of assets might not raise enough funds. • Selling assets to others may increase competition.

External sources

Family and friends

This is a popular source of finance for people setting up a business.

Benefits	Problems
• Interest rates may be low as family members may be reluctant to charge interest. • The time to repay the loan may be unlimited, for close family members. • Family members are unlikely to want to take over the business.	• The amount available may be limited, if family savings are low • Family members may need to be repaid urgently, so repayment could be asked for with little notice. • Family members are less likely to want to see a business plan, so details about the likely success of the business are not carefully considered.

New partners

A business might invite someone to join the company as a new partner, in return for providing some finance.

Benefits	Problems
• More money will be brought into the business. • No interest will be paid on that money. • The skills and qualities of the new partner may help to increase the business's profits.	• The amounts of new finance contributed may be limited. • A new partner will have an input on decision making, reducing the control of estabilshed partners, potentially affecting the business negatively. • The new partner may not be welcomed by existing partners, who may receive lower profits.

Share issue

Companies can sell shares in return for a payment. Those who buy the shares are called **shareholders** and own a part of the company. A share issue is the sale of new shares to new or existing shareholders.

Benefits	Problems
• Vast sums of money can be raised, particularly for shares sold on the Stock Exchange. • Shareholders have limited liability. • The money does not have to be repaid by the business. Shareholders can sell their shares to other investors, but the business is not affected. • Interest is not paid on the money.	• It is expensive to set up a public sale of shares: many legal documents are required. • Shareholders are paid a share of the profits, through **dividends**. • Control of the business may be lost to other shareholders. • New shares may reduce the value of shares, displeasing existing shareholders.

Venture capitalists

Venture capitalists are private investors providing capital to new or small businesses that have the potential for growth.

Benefits	Problem
• Venture capitalists are experienced in owning and running businesses. • The can share their advice, experiences and business contacts.	• Venture capitalists may want control over the business for which they are providing finance.

> **Venture capitalists** are wealthy people or organisations that provide finance to businesses that are thought to be risky.
>
> **Business angels** are wealthy individuals who invest their private capital in start-up businesses in return for a share in the business.

Business angels

Business angels provide relatively small amounts of money to new business. The advantages and disadvantages of business angels are similar to those for venture capitalists.

Bank loans

Businesses can borrow fixed sums of money from a bank for a fixed period. These are called **bank loans**.

Benefits	Problems

• Interest rates:
  – may be fixed at the start of the loan, so there is certainty about its cost
  – may be lower than other forms of borrowing.
• Businesses have a long time to repay the loans.
• Loans are suitable for borrowing large sums of money.
• Goods purchased with the loan become the property of the business immediately.
• The loan will not affect the ownership of the business.
	• Banks will be selective about the type of business given a loan.
	• It can take time to receive a loan as the bank will want to see the business plan to ensure whether the business will be able to repay it.
	• The bank may want **collateral** security (something of equivalent value to the loan, such as a mortgage) that will be taken by the bank if the loan is not repaid.
	• Failure to repay a loan could lead to the business being closed or, in the case of sole traders or partnerships, the owners may lose their personal assets.

Bank loans are long- to medium-term sources of finance that can be used to buy producer goods.

Collateral is an asset that a bank holds as security for the repayment of a loan.

Overdrafts give entrepreneurs and businesses the right to borrow variable amounts of money up to an agreed limit.

Cash flow is the money that flows into and out of a business on a day-to-day basis.

Trade credit is a period that suppliers allow customers before payment for supplies must be made.

Overdrafts

Overdrafts are short-term loans provided by banks to cover a business's **cash flow** difficulties. The business can withdraw more from its bank account than is currently in it, and repay the overdraft by putting money back in to their account.

Benefits	Problems
• Interest is only paid on the overdrawn amount. • They are usually for small amounts and for the short term, to pay for day-to-day expenses. • New agreements do not need to be made with the bank every time the business becomes overdrawn.	• The rate of interest is usually higher than found on bank loans. • Overdrafts can be ended at any time if the bank is not happy with the way the business is being run, or is uncertain about whether debts can be repaid. This will sometimes bring about the end of the business. • As they are short term and for small amounts of money, overdrafts are not suitable for the purchase of capital goods.

Trade credit

Trade credit is a system of interest-free short-term credit for the purchase of non-durable goods. These will need to be paid for, usually within one month.

Benefits	Problems
• The business can buy goods and will have time to process these, or sell on, before having to pay for them. This will enable a quick profit. • No interest is paid on the credit.	• It is a very short-term form of finance. • The amounts credited will be small.

Tip

Do not assume that interest is not paid on overdrafts.

Now test yourself

TESTED

1. Outline two advantages to a business of borrowing money from family members.
2. Suggest a reason why taking on additional partners may cause problems for a business.
3. Outline one advantage to a business of taking out a bank loan to finance expansion.
4. What is meant by the term collateral security?
5. Why would an overdraft not be suitable for a business wanting to expand its factory?
6. How is trade credit a valuable source of finance for local shopkeepers?

Now test yourself and exam practice answers at www.hoddereducation.co.uk/myrevisionnotesdownloads

Hire purchase

Hire purchase is a loan from a finance company for the business to buy a specific item, such as a piece of machinery. The borrower pays a deposit and can use the machine while renting it from the lender. Once a final payment has been made the equipment belongs to the borrower.

Benefits	Problems
● The item can be used immediately. ● Instalments are paid regularly using the income generated by the business. ● The equipment will eventually be owned by the business. ● The equipment can be returned to the borrower during the repayment period with no effect on the liabilities of the business owners.	● Interest rates tend to be higher than if the assets were bought using a bank loan. ● The asset is not owned until completely paid for. ● The asset can be taken back by the lender if instalments are missed. This could threaten the existence of the business.

> **Hire purchase** is a system of credit whereby the borrower pays a deposit to be able to use a good for a set period. During this time instalments are paid to cover the cost of the good plus interest.
>
> **Leasing** is a system of renting an asset to a business. The asset remains the property of the business renting out the good.

Leasing

Benefits	Problems
● The business does not have to raise finance to pay the full cost of an asset to be able to use it. ● Maintenance and repair costs are paid by the owner of the asset, rather than the business. ● Updated equipment will be provided by the owner of the asset, so the business can take advantage of advances in technology.	● The asset does not belong to the business. ● Regular rental payments must be made to be able to use the equipment. ● The rental company must pay for the equipment (and its maintenance) to earn its own profit, so payments tend to be higher than for other sources of finance.

Government grants

There is a range of grants provided by local, regional and national governments as well as the European Union to persuade businesses to settle in a locality (usually an area with high levels of unemployment, but the potential for growth). Businesses must pay some of the costs but local councils, regional authorities, such as those in London and Manchester, and national parliaments, such as those in Cardiff and Westminster, will make contributions.

Benefits	Problems
● Grants cut the costs of setting up in certain regions as businesses do not have to find finance from other sources. ● The money is a grant so it does not have to be repaid. ● There are no interest charges.	● A complicated application process with many forms and questioning by Government officials. Governments will want to be satisfied that jobs are likely to be created. ● The business will have to set up in the area specified by the Government. ● There will be much publicity before and after the grant has been awarded with the public, the media and politicians wanting to ensure that the taxpayer's money has been well spent.

Now test yourself

TESTED ☐

1 What is meant by the term hire purchase?
2 Outline one disadvantage for a business using hire purchase to buy machinery.
3 Explain one difference between hire purchase and leasing.
4 Why are some businesses reluctant to apply for government grants as a source of finance?

The suitability of the different sources of finance

The source of finance used by businesses will depend on their circumstances.

Business start-up

- **Owner's capital**. Entrepreneurs will be willing to use their own savings.
- **Family and friends** will often give financial support to new businesses.
- **Share issue**. New private limited companies will sell shares to investors acceptable to existing shareholders.
- **Business angels** will provide financial support to new enterprises if they feel they have potential for growth.
- **Bank loans** will be available if the bank believes the business will survive and be able to repay the loans. Decisions will be made on the strength of the business plan.
- **Hire purchase** will enable the business to buy equipment when bank loans are not available. If the business fails to repay, the equipment must be returned.
- **Leasing** can be used as an alternative to hire purchase, but the equipment is never owned by the business.
- **Government grants** will be available to **start-up businesses** if it is believed that the business has potential for growth and if jobs are likely to be created.

A **start-up business** is one that has been recently established.

Cash flow issues

Cash flow is the difference between the inflow and outflow of cash. Businesses with no cash will not be able to buy materials nor pay their workers so production stops. Finance may be needed to cover short-term debts. The most suitable sources include:

- **Owner's capital**. Owners will use personal savings to cover short-term debts of the business.
- Similarly, with **family and friends**.
- **Bank overdrafts** are ideal for short-term cash flow issues. Bills can be paid even if the business has no money in its account.
- **Trade credit** helps the business buy materials without having the cash immediately. Payments can be made after goods have been sold.

Expansion

Existing businesses are more likely to have a better financial reputation than start-up businesses. The suitability of the different sources of finance for expansion will be the same as those starting up. In addition, there are:

- **retained profits**. Businesses with the aim of expansion will use past profits for investment in the business.
- **selling assets**. Businesses that have been in existence for some time will have accumulated assets that they no longer need. These can be sold to buy any new equipment needed.
- **share issue**. Existing businesses are more likely to be public limited companies, which can sell shares to anyone on the Stock Exchange and so are able to gain more finance.
- **bank loans** will be more easily obtained by existing businesses looking to expand because of their reputation and because they are able to provide more detailed business plans.

Now test yourself

1. Suggest why many entrepreneurs must rely on external finance when starting a business.
2. Why are business angels willing to finance start-up businesses?
3. Why aren't retained profits used to finance cash flow problems when businesses start up?
4. Explain which assets businesses will be able to sell to finance other investments.

TESTED

Revenue and costs

Revenue, costs, profit and loss

REVISED

Revenue is the amount of money a business takes from customers when selling its goods. Total revenue is calculated with the formula:

Total revenue = selling **price** × number of goods sold

Costs are what a business pays to produce goods and services and to run the business. There are two types of costs.

- **Fixed costs** must be paid whether the business produces one good or a million goods. The money is used to pay for rent for buildings, cost of buying machinery or payments for insurance. The more goods that are produced, the lower the fixed cost per good produced.
- **Variable costs** will change as more goods are being produced and as more resources are used. It is calculated with the formula:
  Variable cost = variable cost of producing one good × number of goods produced
- **Total cost** can be calculated by adding together all the costs of production with the formula:
  Total cost = fixed cost + variable cost
- **Profit** is an important aim of all businesses. To make a profit the enterprise must take in more money than it spends.

> **Tip**
>
> It is important to be precise in using the term profit: stating 'money made' can be confusing and may not be credited with marks.

The formula for calculating profit is:

Profit = total revenue − total cost

A **loss** occurs when the business spends more than it earns. Short-term losses can be covered by past profits but too many losses will threaten the survival of the business.

The calculations

A business might have fixed costs of £100 per day. It manufactures a product that costs £5 per good for resources and that sells for £7 per good. The result is as follows:

No. of goods	Fixed cost (FC)	Variable cost (VC)	Total cost FC + VC	Total revenue (TR)	Profit/loss TR – TC
0	100	£0	£100	£0	−£100
10	100	£50	£150	£70	−£80
20	100	£100	£200	£140	−£60
30	100	£150	£250	£210	−£40
40	100	£200	£300	£280	−£20
50	100	£250	£350	£350	£0
60	100	£300	£400	£420	£20
70	100	£350	£450	£490	£40
80	100	£400	£500	£560	£60

> **Tip**
>
> There are several terms and formulae that must be learned in this topic.

Total revenue is the full amount of money taken in by a business when selling all its goods in a period.

Price is the amount a business asks a customer to pay for a single product.

Costs are the spending that is necessary to set up and run a business.

Fixed costs are those costs that do not alter when a business changes its output.

Variable costs are the costs that vary directly with the business's level of output.

Total cost is the full amount of money spent by a business when producing the goods sold in a period.

Profit is the difference between the total revenue of a business and the total costs of a business, when revenue is greater than cost.

Loss is the amount by which a business's costs are larger than its revenue from all sales.

Now test yourself

Use the table to answer the following questions:

1. Explain why the business makes a loss of £100 when no goods are being produced or sold.
2. How many goods need to be produced for the business to make no profit and no loss?

TESTED

Break-even?

When a business is making neither a profit nor a loss it is breaking even. Knowing the **break-even** can help a business better understand its costs, revenue and potential profit, and then use this information to inform business decisions. The level of output where this happens can be shown in a **break-even chart** or in a contribution calculation (see below).

Break-even charts

The figures previously shown can be plotted on a break-even chart as illustrated:

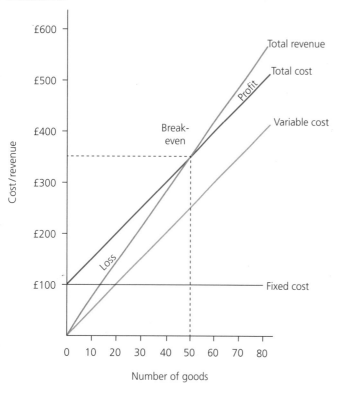

Figure 4.1 **A break-even chart**

> **Break-even** is the level of production at which a business's total costs and total revenue from sales are equal.
>
> A **break-even chart** shows a business's costs and revenues and the level of production needed to break even.

The lines on this chart were drawn in the order:
1 **Fixed costs**. As these do not change with output they are shown as a horizontal line.
2 **Variable costs**. As variable costs are not paid if no goods are produced, the line starts at the origin but it rises steadily as output increases.
3 **Total costs**. This line shows the addition of fixed costs and variable costs so it rises steadily as output increases.
4 **Total revenue**. As total revenue is zero when no sales are made, the line starts at the origin but it rises steadily as output increases.

Interpreting the chart

- Break-even is reached where total cost is the same as total revenue. In this case, it is at a level of 50 sales: the break-even level of output.
- Fewer sales than break-even means that a loss has been made.
- More sales than break-even means that a profit has been made.
- Whether a profit or loss has been made, the vertical distance between the total cost and the total revenue lines will show the level of the profit or loss.

> **Tip**
>
> In questions that ask for an interpretation of a break-even chart remember to state the output (50 sales here) rather than reading the cost / revenue axis (£350 in this case).

Calculate break-even through contribution

An alternative way of finding break-even is by calculating the **contribution** each good sold makes towards the fixed costs. To find the break-even level of output the following formula is used:

Break-even output = fixed costs / **contribution per unit**

Or

Break-even output = fixed cost / (selling price − variable cost)

In the previous example this would be:

Break-even output = 100 / (7 − 5) = 50

i.e. the same answer when read from the break-even chart.

> **Contribution** is sales revenue minus variable costs of production.
>
> **Contribution per unit** is sales revenue minus variable costs of production divided by the number of units of output.

Now test yourself

Alison has set up a juice bar in a busy town centre location for which her fixed costs are £1000 per week. Each plastic glass of juice, which sells for £3, costs her £2 to produce. Alison wants to find how many drinks she will need to sell to make a profit.
1 What is meant by variable cost? Give an example of a variable cost product used by Alison.
2 What is meant by fixed cost? Give an example of a fixed cost Alison might pay.
3 Explain the meaning of contribution.
4 Calculate how many glasses of juice Alison will need to sell per week to break even.

Changes in break-even

A break-even point is not fixed. A change in costs and prices can impact the profits made by a business, and so alter the break-even.
- A rise in price will mean that the business will need to sell fewer goods to be able to cover its costs and to break even, or to increase its profits. (This assumes that customers are still willing to buy at the higher price.)
- A rise in fixed costs – perhaps because of an increase in rents – will mean that break-even will involve the need to sell more goods.
- A rise in variable costs will again mean that more goods will need to be sold to break even.

> **Tip**
>
> Even though they are called fixed costs, such costs can rise or fall over time and so the line can move up or down.

Evaluation of break-even analysis

Benefits	Problems
• It helps businesses to decide whether it is worthwhile to provide a good or service. • It guides businesses when making decisions, such as whether to increase price or on issues to do with costs.	• It can be difficult to estimate the contribution certain costs make to the cost of producing an individual good – particularly when the business produces a variety of products. • It assumes that price is constant but, in a competitive market, prices may change.

The use of profit as a reward for business investment

Break-even analysis shows the importance of profit to all businesses. Within this fixed costs are a major consideration and the bulk of these costs involve investment by the business. Investment involves:

- buying property such as land and buildings
- buying machinery, equipment and vehicles
- taking over other businesses.

Profits are often the main motivation for an investment, and also determine how successful an investment has been.

Measuring the success of an investment (ARR)

Business owners need to be certain whether it is worthwhile to invest in a project or whether they would be better off keeping their money in an interest-paying account, or in an alternative investment.

To help them in making the decision, they will calculate the **average (or accounting) rate of return (ARR)**. The calculation involves two stages:

1 Calculate the average profit. This is the total profit expected to be earned from an investment and the number of years that investment will be earning profits. So:

Average profit = total net profit / number of years of investment

2 Calculate Average Rate of Return (ARR):

ARR = average profit / initial investment × 100

The result will give a percentage answer. This can be compared with the rates for using the money in alternative ways. If the ARR is higher than elsewhere the investment is more likely to happen.

> **Note**
>
> The topic of ARR is included in the Eduqas Specification but not in the WJEC Specification.

> The **average rate of return (ARR)** compares the average yearly profit from an investment with the cost of the investment and is stated as a percentage.

Now test yourself

1 Why are profits an important source of finance?
2 Suggest two ways in which a business may invest its profits.
3 What is meant by average profit? (Eduqas only)
4 Why is ARR important to a business deciding whether to buy new machinery? (WJEC only)

Profit and loss accounts

The aim of any business is to make as much profit, or the least loss, as possible. Every year businesses draw up a table to show how their profits were achieved. This is the **profit and loss account** or **income statement**.

Main components of a profit and loss account

A profit and loss account is divided into:
- **Sales revenue** or **turnover**. This is the income of the business from the sale of goods and services.
- **Cost of sales**. This will include:
  - the cost of the stock bought to produce goods or to provide the goods for resale
  - the cost of workers directly involved in production
  - the cost of gas and electricity directly used in production.
- **Gross profit**. This is the profit made before other costs are considered.
- **Expenses** or **overheads** are the costs that must be paid whether the business is producing or not. They include:
  - salaries paid to managers and administrative workers
  - insurance premiums
  - rent for the buildings
  - maintenance costs.
- **Net profit** is a measure of the performance of a business by showing how profitable it has been. This profit will then be used to:
  - pay the tax liability of the business to the Government
  - distribute to the owners or as a dividend to shareholders in the case of limited companies
  - be retained by the business for future investment.

> A **profit and loss account** is a financial statement showing a business's sales revenue and costs and thus its profit or loss over a period. Profit and loss accounts are also called **income statements**.
>
> **Sales revenue** or **turnover** is the amount of money taken in by a business when selling a good or service.
>
> **Gross profit** is the profit made before expenses have been paid.
>
> **Net profit** is the final profit made by a business after all costs have been paid.

Construct, calculate and interpret a profit and loss account

The main components of a profit and loss account are used during the calculation as in Figure 4.2.

Below is an example of a profit and loss account:

Border Foods plc	
Profit and loss account for the year	
Sales revenue	£1 500 000
Cost of sales	(£500 000)
Gross profit	£1 000 000
Expenses	(£50 000)
Net profit	£950 000

↙ remember

Sales revenue or turnover	£1 500 000
minus	–
Cost of sales	£500 000
equals	=
Gross profit	£1 000 000
minus	–
Expenses or overheads	£50 000
equals	=
Net profit	£950 000

Figure 4.2 A profit and loss flow diagram

sales revenue − cost of sale
= gross profit

gross profit − expenses
= net profit.

1 What is the turnover of a business?
2 Suggest two expenses that a business might have.

The importance of the profit and loss accounts

To businesses

Businesses will use profit and loss accounts to make comparisons and as an aid to decide whether the business has been a success. These comparisons will be based on:

- **Targets**. The aims and objectives of the business will set targets on expected revenue, costs and profits. Current profit and loss accounts will show whether these targets are being reached.
- **Time**. If higher profits are earned from one year to the next this will be a success. If the current profit is less than in previous years, plans will need to be put in place to correct the situation.
- **Competitor** profit or loss. How does this business compare with others in the same market? For many companies, this information is publicly available.

Worse than expected results will lead to the business taking action, perhaps by:

- increasing advertising to boost sales and so increase revenues
- increasing prices
- purchasing cheaper materials to reduce the cost of sales
- reducing expenses by cutting back on the number of administrative workers or on advertising.

To stakeholders

- **Shareholders** will want to know whether the business has been profitable as this will affect their dividend and may affect the value of their shares. They will also want to know whether the business is likely to survive.
- **Managers** will want to see whether the business has been profitable, as the figures show whether they have been effective in controlling business costs and encouraging sales. Results may affect their salaries and bonuses and may impact on job security.
- **Workers** will want to know the profitability of a business, as this may impact on negotiations for wage increases and may also determine whether they keep their jobs.
- **Customers** may want to know whether higher prices have led to higher profits. Business customers may want to know whether the business is likely to continue to supply materials or goods.
- **Suppliers** may want to know about survival of their customers, to ensure markets can be maintained and debts paid.
- **Banks** (as the suppliers of finance) will want to decide whether to lend money and whether the business is likely to be able to repay its loans and overdraft.
- **Competitors** will be interested to make their own comparisons and to plan their own strategies.
- The **Government** will want to know how much tax will be collected from the business, or to decide whether actions are needed to control excessive profits.
- **Local communities** will want to know about the profits and the use of these profits to reduce the environmental impact on their communities.

Now test yourself

1 Why is a comparison of profits over time important to the business when setting objectives?
2 How will shareholders be affected by lower than expected profits?
3 Why might workers be pleased to see a rise in profits over several years?
4 Why are competitors keen to know the profit and loss figures for rival businesses?

TESTED

Gross and net profit margins

Gross and net profits by themselves are not enough to make comparisons between businesses. It would be expected that larger businesses with greater sales will make greater profits. To make it easier to compare, businesses will calculate the profit as a percentage of sales.

Gross profit margin (GPM)

The **gross profit margin** is calculated with the following formula. The answer is shown as a percentage.

GPM = gross profit / sales revenue × 100

Net profit margin (NPM)

The **net profit margin** is a better indicator of a business's financial performance than gross profit margin as its calculation includes all the costs paid by a business. NPM is calculated with the following formula. The answer is shown as a percentage.

NPM = net profit / sales revenue × 100

> **Gross profit margin** is the gross profit expressed as a percentage of sales.
>
> **Net profit margin** is the net profit expressed as a percentage of sales.

Improving profits and reducing costs

The profit and loss account shows that a business can increase its profit or reduce its loss by increasing its sales revenue and cutting its costs. However, doing so may have consequences for other parts of the business.

Aim	Action taken	Possible consequence
Increase sales revenue	Increase advertising and promotion to encourage people to buy.	Marketing may be expensive and will add to costs.
	Increase the price of goods.	Sales may fall due which, if the fall is great enough, will cause sales revenue to also fall.
	Reduce the price of goods.	Sales will have to increase a lot for sales revenue to increase.
Cut costs	Buy lower quality materials.	This will reduce the quality of the finished product, so sales may fall.
	Buy materials in greater bulk to take advantage of bulk discounts.	The materials will need to be stored, adding to warehousing costs.
	Cut wages and salaries of workers.	This will reduce the quality and morale of workers so: ● a poorer quality service will be provided and ● customers will be lost and sales revenue reduced.
	Introduce technology to reduce the number of workers.	Workers become less motivated because of the threats to their jobs. In shops, many customers do not like the automated tills.
	Move to a different location where rents may be cheaper.	Moving costs may be high. The new location may be less convenient for customers.
	Reduce spending on maintenance of equipment and refurbishment of buildings.	Machinery will break down more often, affecting production and possibly sales. The life of machinery will be reduced, so expensive replacements will be needed. Poorly decorated buildings may put off customers.

Now test yourself

1 How does the figure for net profit differ from that of net profit margin?
2 What effect will increased use of machinery to cut costs have on employees?

Cash flow

The importance of cash to a business

The definitions of **cash** and profit are clearly different.

- **Cash** is money that is available to use quickly as notes and coins within the business, or as deposits in bank accounts.
- **Profit** is the surplus at the end of a trading period used to:
  ○ reward the owners of the business
  ○ plough back into longer-term investments in the business.

> **Cash** is money that is available to a business to spend immediately. It normally includes notes and coins as well as money in bank accounts.

Cash-flow forecast

Cash in a business is always changing.

- Customers pay for goods and services bought so cash increases.
- Businesses pay their debts so cash decreases.

Cash is therefore said to flow into and out of a business.

A **cash-flow forecast** is a **prediction** of a business's future cash inflows and outflows. Estimates of **cash flow** are important because:

- When a business is set up, the owners will want to know whether they are likely to have enough cash to pay for their day-to-day needs.
- If the business wants to borrow money, the bank will want to know that the business can pay its short-term debts and repay loans.

In each case the business should construct a cash-flow forecast.

> A **cash-flow forecast** sets out a business's expected inflows and outflows of cash over a period.
>
> **Cash flow** is the money that flows into and out of a business on a day-to-day basis.

Constructing, calculating and interpreting a cash-flow forecast

A cash-flow forecast is written for each month for several months. It is divided into three sections:

1 **Cash inflow** is the money predicted to enter the business over the month and is made up of:
   ○ the savings of the owners invested into the business
   ○ bank loans received from banks and investors
   ○ expected sales revenue.
2 **Cash outflow** is the money the business estimates it will spend each month. It is made up of:
   ○ the cost of materials paid to suppliers
   ○ payments for advertising
   ○ wages paid to workers
   ○ rent or mortgage repayments for the property
   ○ interest paid to banks for loans
   ○ taxes on the income of owners or on sales paid to the Government.
3 **Net cash flow** is the difference between the cash estimated to be coming into the business and the cash predicted to be leaving the business in the month. It is calculated with:
   Net cash flow = cash inflow − cash outflow

A business estimates how much cash it expects to have at the end of each month by adding or subtracting its net cash flow to/from its **opening balance** (the amount estimated to be in the account at the start of the month). The answer gives the **closing balance** for the end of the month, which then becomes the **opening balance** for the next month.

For example, Janice Taylor operates a pleasure boat business at a seaside during the summer months. Her cash-flow forecast is shown below.

	Apr	May	Jun	Jul	Aug	Sept
Receipts	£	£	£	£	£	£
Expected turnover	2,000	2,000	4,000	7,000	10,000	4,000
Bank loan	2,000					
Expected inflow	4,000	2,000	4,000	7,000	10,000	4,000
Payments						
Fuel	300	300	400	800	1,000	600
Wages	2,000	2,000	2,000	3,000	4,000	1,500
Advertising	100	100	100	200	200	100
Rent	200	100	200	300	500	200
Other payments	100	100	100	200	200	100
Total outflow	2,700	2,600	2,800	4,500	5,900	2,500
Net cash flow	1,300	(600)	1,200	2,500	4,100	1,500
Opening bank balance	4,000	5,300	4,700	5,900	8,400	12,500
Closing bank balance	5,300	4,700	5,900	8,400	12,500	14,000

Now test yourself

1 Why is cash important to a business?
2 Outline the differences between cash and profit.
3 What is a cash-flow forecast?
4 Why would a bank want to see a cash-flow forecast before making a loan?

TESTED ☐

The impact of cash-flow forecasts

REVISED ☐

On businesses

Businesses will use cash-flow forecasts to estimate the effects of their business decisions. The forecasts will show the business:
- the times they may need an overdraft
- whether it is worthwhile going ahead with a project.

On stakeholders

- **Shareholders** will want to know the effects of business decisions on cash in the business, particularly if they have been asked to make further investments.
- **Managers** will want to see whether their decisions will impact on the cash in the business.
- **Workers** will want to know if there will be occasions when their pay may be delayed.
- **Customers** who have been asked to pay a deposit in advance of receiving goods may be interested in the cash situation of a business.
- **Suppliers** may show an interest when the business is predicting cash-flow issues that might delay the payments of trade credit. This will help them to decide whether to allow such credit.
- **Banks**, as the suppliers of finance, will want to decide whether to lend, whether the business is likely to be able to repay loans, and when it may need an overdraft.

Improving cash-flow issues ★

Aim	Action taken	Benefit	Problem
Increase revenue	Changing prices	This may increase revenue, particularly for increase in the price of necessities.	The effects of a price change on revenue is uncertain, particularly for luxury goods.
	Increasing promotions	This may lead to increased sales.	There may be no impact on sales. They will be expensive, so costs will increase and cash will fall.
Reducing costs	Reducing staff	This will reduce the wages bill.	This may lead to an inferior service or reduced output, leading to A loss of customers, so revenue may fall.
	Buying cheaper materials	This will reduce production costs ... Leading to lower prices, which could Generate more custom producing more cash.	Customers may not be happy about the quality of the product or service so ... Sales and income may fall, leading to a reduction in cash.
	Delaying payment to suppliers	This will allow cash to be used for other purposes.	Suppliers may become reluctant to offer trade credit.
	Chasing-up the debts owed by customers	This may generate the required cash.	This may lead to cash problems for those customers who may not be able to pay their debts.
	Extra funding (usually by extending overdrafts)	This will lead to an immediate increase in cash available.	Overdraft interest rates may be high, so Costs rise and profits fall. Banks can ask for an overdraft to be repaid immediately leading to further cash-flow problems.

Now test yourself

TESTED ☐

1 What is an overdraft and how might one be important to a business?
2 Why might customers be interested in the cash-flow position of a business?
3 What effect might a cut in the number of workers have on the cash flow of a business?
4 Suggest a problem that might arise if a business chases up bad debts to improve cash flow.

Financial performance

Using financial data to analyse business performance

REVISED

4 Finance

Businesses produce data related to revenue, costs, profit, profit and loss accounts and cash flow, and present this in the form of charts, forecasts, reports and business plans. They also gather information provided by other businesses, government organisations and the media.

The information gathered helps businesses to:
- review and analyse what has happened in the past
- estimate what may happen in the future
- make decisions about how the business will progress.

The data gathered will be **qualitative** and **quantitative**.

> **Qualitative data** is information that cannot easily be measured. There are many examples of qualitative financial data. One is the effect on the ethical reputation of a business of a decision to invest in a factory overseas.
>
> **Quantitative data** is data that can be measured and is written as numbers or in the form of a graph. A business's fixed and variable costs are examples of quantitative financial data.

Qualitative data

This is information that describes what people have observed and will often be based on ideas, opinions and beliefs. Such qualitative data is more likely to address:

- **The reputation of the business** as seen publicly in the media or privately with feedback from customers. This can be analysed to find whether the business has been treated favourably, whether this has impacted on revenue, costs and profits and what needs to be done to improve reputation.
- **Environmental and ethical issues**. These are linked to the reputation of the business and the ways in which its practices impact on the natural environment and the treatment of its stakeholders.
- **Responsibilities to employees**. These require that businesses look at the welfare of their workers and at how decisions to cut costs may impact on them.

The nature of qualitative data means that it is often biased and cannot be measured.

Quantitative data

This information includes numerical data that has quantities and values. The information can be easily analysed and interpreted. All of the financial data you have been shown in this chapter so far has been quantitative data.

Analysis of quantitative information involves counting, calculating and measuring what has been recorded in the past in order to estimate what will probably happen in the future. The data will be compared over time, or with other businesses and with forecasts. Businesses will look at:

- The **extent** of any differences by considering:
  ○ Is one number higher than another? This may be shown in a bar graph.
  ○ What is the difference between the two numbers?
  ○ What is the percentage difference or effect as shown by profit margins and ARR?

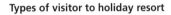

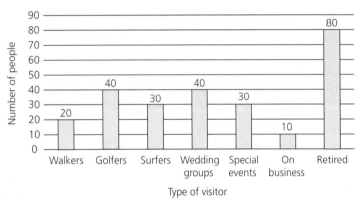

Figure 4.3 A bar chart

- The **proportion** of one figure in relation to others, such as in market share. This can involve the use of pie charts. If the entire market grows, a bigger pie chart can be shown alongside.
- The **trend**. Are revenues, costs or profits rising or falling? These can be shown by a line graph. The business can then base decisions on what to do about the trend. Results different from the trend can also be shown.

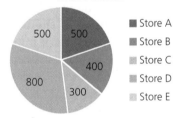

Figure 4.4 A pie chart

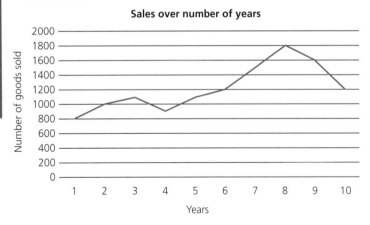

Figure 4.5 A line graph

- Is the data **consistent**? Are indicators of a healthy cash flow in the future reflected in current profit and loss accounts?

5 Marketing

Identifying and understanding customers

The importance of identifying and understanding customers

Businesses exist to make a profit. This profit is made by ensuring that costs are kept as low as possible and that revenue is as high as possible. Businesses can have some control over costs but revenues are influenced by whether customers are willing to buy the goods and services. It is important that businesses identify who their customers are and to understand what they are likely to buy. This is the job of the Marketing Department of a business. Understanding customers helps businesses to continue to produce and sell their products, to maintain and even increase prices and to keep the reputation of the business to ensure future success.

Successful businesses will not only identify what customers want, they will also try to influence the actions of customers in order to persuade them to buy products. These customers will be found in different groups or **market segments**.

> A **market segment** is a group of similar needs within the overall market.

How markets are segmented

Markets can be divided according to:
- **Age**. A business will offer products that appeal to certain ages.
- **Gender**. Some products are aimed at men, some at women, and some will be adapted to appeal to both genders.
- **Geographic**. Markets can be segmented according to where the customer lives as different areas have different tastes and preferences.
- **Income**. People who earn different amounts of money will buy more expensive or cheaper products, so businesses will offer a range of products at different prices.
- **Lifestyle**. A person's lifestyle includes their attitudes and habits, interests and hobbies.
- **Ethnic background and religion**. Some goods and services are aimed at racial or religious segments of the market.

Why segment the market?

By dividing the market into segments businesses:
- produce goods and services to meet the needs of individual consumers
- promote and advertise their products to customers in the right places
- charge a price matched to the customers' ability to pay.

Some businesses will aim their goods and services at the mass market, where most people will be interested in buying their products. Others will target specific market segments to appeal to smaller groups of customers. Dividing the market will therefore affect:
- the types of goods and services produced
- the design, colours and packaging of products
- the volume of sales of products
- the prices at which goods and services are sold
- the scale of production
- the profits of the business
- where the products are marketed and advertised.

Now test yourself

1 Why is it important for businesses to identify who their customers are?
2 Explain what is meant by the term market segment.
3 How is an individual's income likely to affect the type of goods bought?
4 How does market segment influence where and when a business advertises its products?

Market research

The importance of market research

Businesses can operate without knowing what their customers want and what is provided by the rest of the market. However, such businesses are likely to fail as they may be producing goods and services that no one wants. **Market research** is concerned with finding out information about the market in which a business operates. This information will enable businesses to make decisions that are more likely to lead to success. Market research will gather information from:

- **customers** to find:
  - personal information, to find the market segment they purchase in
  - which goods and services they buy, to decide whether there is a market for products
  - why they want to buy these goods and services
  - ways of persuading people to buy
  - which products they may like to buy, to see whether it is worthwhile developing new products.
- **competitors** to find:
  - the number of competitors
  - how much of the market competitors control
  - the type of competitors, such as their history and strength of the brands
  - their scale of operation, indicating the level of their costs and profits
  - whether they are growing businesses or not.
- **market trends** to estimate whether sales are likely to grow.

Market research will help businesses to:
- find opportunities in the market
- consider what they can do to meet these opportunities
- decide whether past advertising and promotions have succeeded.

> **Market research** is the process of gathering, analysing and processing data relevant to marketing decisions.
>
> **Primary** or **field research** uses data gathered for the first time.
>
> **Secondary** or **desk research** uses data that has been gathered already.

How is market research carried out?

Market research involves collecting, presenting and analysing information.

- **Collecting information** involves:
  - **primary** or **field research**, to find information for a specific purpose
  - **secondary** or **desk research**, using information that already exists.
- **Presenting information** means showing the collected information in a way that makes it accurate but easy to understand. Presentation may involve a written report, including qualitative and qualitative data set out in words, tables, graphs and diagrams.
- **Analysing** information involves looking at what the data mean so that owners and managers can be helped to:
  - understand the market to find how it is segmented and who is buying which products
  - find gaps in the market where few other businesses are providing goods and services, so these gaps can be exploited by the business
  - choose between several business strategies
  - make better decisions to ensure resources are not wasted in producing goods few people want
  - determine whether past decisions and actions have been successful.

> **Tip**
>
> Look at the section on Finance to see how this data may be displayed.

> **Now test yourself**
>
> 1 What is meant by the term market research?
> 2 Outline the three stages of market research.
>
> TESTED

Primary and secondary research methods

Primary research

Primary research involves the business gathering new information. This can be done with surveys, focus groups, consumer panels and observation.

Surveys are way of gathering detailed information on a defined subject by questioning a sample of people. Types of survey can vary, but most are based around written questionnaires or interviews.

- **Interviews** often take the form of a questionnaire, but can be more in depth and wide ranging.
  - ○ **Personal, face-to-face interview**. These are held in person between the interviewer and the person being surveyed.

Benefits	Problems
• The interviewer can help people to understand the questions. • They will clearly fill out the responses to the questions.	• They are expensive to carry out. • They can take time to complete.

  - ○ **Telephone interview**. In this case the interviewer asks questions over the telephone.

Benefit	Problems
• They allow a wide geographical area to be covered.	• They can be expensive as researchers call many homes. • The response rate is low as people do not like being disturbed at home.

- **Questionnaires** once drafted can be sent to multiple people.
  - ○ **Postal survey**, sent through the mail.

Benefit	Problems
• Surveys are cheap to carry out.	• The response rate is low as people do not return questionnaires. • Questions must be short, so detailed questions are difficult to ask. • Questionnaires must be well designed and easy to understand.

  - ○ **Internet survey** is completed online.

Benefits	Problems
• They are cheap to carry out. • They allow a wide area to be covered.	• Questionnaires must be well designed and easy to understand. • The response rate is low.

Focus groups are small groups of people selected to give their views on a particular business issue. The group discuss goods and services, and participants offer their opinions so that businesses will have some idea of what the public thinks of new products.

> **Focus groups** are consumers brought together by businesses to discuss their reactions to products before they are launched.

Benefits	Problems
• They give an opportunity to discuss a range of issues. • They can bring to light issues which hadn't previously been considered.	• Focus groups may not represent the market as they involve only a few people. • Results tend to produce opinions, but the small number of people involved makes it difficult to extend their views to the market. • May be expensive to set up in relation to the amount of data obtained.

Consumer panels are groups of consumers within a specific market who have been selected to represent the entire market. They are asked to comment on things such as product design, branding and advertising. Businesses will often make improvements to their products and marketing because of panel recommendations. The benefits and problems of consumer panels are like those of focus groups.

> **Consumer panels** are recruited by research companies to represent the views of consumers in a sector.

Observation involves watching consumers and recording their actions. For example, a business might count how many people enter their shops, and also observe how they shop. This can help businesses to decide where to place goods within the shop.

Benefits	Problems
• Results are based on what consumers are actually doing. • The use of technology means that customers can be counted by sensors.	• Systems may be expensive to set up. • Results show what consumers are doing rather than their motives, so it may be more difficult to develop meaningful marketing strategies.

Secondary research

Secondary (or 'desk') research involves using existing information. Some research will already have been carried out by other businesses, individuals and groups and the Government, so there would be no point in repeating it.

Secondary research may be from:
- **Internal sources**, such as financial and sales information found in the businesses accounts, records of the business, and previous annual reports.
- **External sources**, such as:
  - **Government sources**, for example the Office for National Statistics. These will show economic, business and population trends.

Benefit	Problem
• Research will provide informative data about the market.	• Research will not necessarily meet the specific needs of the business.

  - **the internet**, which contains of a vast range of data that can be found on media websites (general or business-specific news), websites of businesses that carry out their own research and then sell it on to others, and other company websites.

Benefit	Problem
• The research may be informative about the market and competitors.	• It may be biased according to the opinions of the media or the businesses carrying out the research.

  - **competitor information**, found in published annual company reports.

Benefit	Problem
• Annual reports are legal requirements, so the data should be accurate.	• Data may not be easily applied to other business because of difference in business structures and scales of operation.

  - **newspapers and magazines**. There are some that specialise in reporting on the business world and the economy. Some newspapers have reputations for accurate, honest and reliable data but others do not. Some businesses will employ workers to read newspapers and the internet to find relevant data. It will be up to businesses to determine the reliability between the various media.

Now test yourself

1 What is meant by the term field research?
2 Suggest two sources of information for a business carrying out field research.
3 Why are businesses using more online surveys to research the market?
4 Outline one advantage and one disadvantage of using focus groups.

TESTED

Evaluation of primary and secondary research

Primary

Benefits	Problems
• Information specific to the business or the market is gathered. • The information is up to date. • Data is more reliable, especially when it is gathered by specialist research businesses.	• Field research can be expensive to carry out particularly for large-scale surveys. • Field research is very time-consuming. • The results from a sample of consumers may not reflect the full market as people do not have the time or inclination to complete surveys.

Secondary

Benefits	Problems
• The data can be gathered quickly from readily available information • and from many sources. • It is cheap to gather with employees carrying out the research as part of their daily jobs.	• The data may not be exactly what the business wants as it may be too general and not related to the business. • The information may be out of date and may not indicate current market demand and trends.

Market research in different market contexts

The size of the business will determine which type of market research can be afforded and which is required.

	Primary	Secondary
Large businesses	Can afford to employ specialist research companies Can research large – even worldwide – markets	Can afford to employ workers to monitor secondary information about the market
Small businesses	Cannot afford extensive market research May use in-shop surveys and questionnaires Generally only need to consider local areas	Will use desk research gained from the media and the internet

Limitations of market research

Accurate and up-to-date marketing research can be of great value to a business finding what its customers want. This will help the business to gain and keep an advantage over its competitors. However, the benefits may not be gained because:

• Gathering up-to-date data is expensive. Businesses may have to rely on data that is not ideal but that is more cheaply obtained from secondary sources.
• Decisions may have to be taken quickly but market research takes time to gather.
• Data may not be reliable. Perhaps the wrong questions were asked to the wrong people by biased researchers. This may lead to poor decision making and expensive mistakes being made.

> **Note**
>
> Information on qualitative and quantitative data and the use of tables, graphs and charts can be found on pages 65–66.

Now test yourself

TESTED ☐

1 What is meant by the term desk research?
2 Suggest two sources of information for a business carrying out desk research.
3 Why are businesses cautious about using secondary data provided by a rival business?
4 Why would a business prefer to rely on primary data rather than secondary data?

The marketing mix

The four Ps

The **marketing mix** involves the four factors that must be considered when marketing a good or service. As all four factors begin with P, they are known as the **four Ps**.
- **Product**. The right product satisfies customer needs.
- **Price**. The right price is the one customers are willing to pay.
- **Promotion**. Promotion is used to inform and persuade customers to buy your product.
- **Place**. Make it easy for the customer to buy your product by putting it in the right place.

The four Ps must be applied in the right mix for the business to succeed. A business will combine all elements of the marketing mix to develop a marketing strategy, and each business's marketing mix will be different, depending on the product and the size of the business.

Product

Products provided by different manufacturers may be similar, but businesses will need to highlight any differences in design and other features, for example reliability or durability, or ethically and environmentally considered elements. Businesses may offer slightly different products to cater for customer demands and competitive pressures.

Price

The **price** of the product must reflect:
- The cost of producing a good or service, and the profit needed to persuade the business to supply products. Businesses will want to sell at high prices.
- The monetary value customers place on the product. They want to buy at low prices although they will buy expensive goods if they believe the price is worth it.

Promotion

Promotion involves:
- making potential customers aware that:
  - products are available
  - there are special offers and other promotions
- explaining what the product is and what it looks like
- making customers aware of what the product does
- persuading them to buy the product.

Place

Traditionally customers have bought goods at shops, markets and through mail order. The internet has allowed them to buy goods from wider markets without the need to travel to shops.

> The **marketing mix** refers to all the activities influencing whether a customer buys a product.
>
> **Product** is the good or service provided by a business.
>
> **Price** is the amount of money a business wants to receive to sell a good or service, or the amount of money the consumer is willing to pay to buy that product.
>
> **Promotion** involves information and techniques used by businesses to make consumers aware of products and to persuade them to buy those products.
>
> **Place** is where the product is available for the consumer to purchase.

The marketing mix and business departments

In businesses, responsibility for marketing is taken by the Marketing Department but it cannot operate in isolation from other departments. All departments in the business are informed by, and help to implement, the marketing mix.

- The **Operations** Department will need to ensure that goods are produced in a way that reflects the marketing mix to satisfy customer expectations. It must also have products available to meet demands.
- The **Finance** Department will need to be satisfied that the marketing costs are justified and that they are covered in the price of the products.
- The **Sales** Department will organise the distribution of goods.

> **Note**
>
> For more detail on these departments see the section on Human Resources.

Changing the marketing mix

Over time the marketing mix of a business will change in line with the changing aims and objectives of the business, and in response to competitive pressures.

- **Product** design will be updated in response to changes in consumer needs and wants.
- **Price** will be affected by changes in costs, consumer incomes and competitor pricing.
- **Promotion** will be affected by consumer use of advertising media.
- **Place** will alter because of changes in consumer habits and distribution methods.

How the marketing mix will differ for different types and sizes of businesses

The marketing mix will be different for every business. Some will place greater emphasis on the product than on price; some will want to be selling in the right place rather than spending too much on promotion. The size of the business often determines how it uses the marketing mix.

Now test yourself

1. What is meant by the term marketing mix?
2. How can businesses show their products to be different from their competitors?
3. Why is price important to the customer and to the producer?
4. How is the marketplace changing for consumers?

TESTED

	Small businesses	Large businesses
Product	• Most small shops have no impact on the type, brands and packaging of goods being produced. • Those involved in job production will assist customers in producing goods to match individual requirements.	• Large shops can order goods from manufacturers to the specific designs of the shopkeeper. • These will often be sold as own brand goods. • For mass produced goods, opportunities to change the product will be limited.
Price	• Price is determined by the supplier. Small businesses cannot buy in bulk to be able to pass on price reductions to their customers.	• Operating on a large scale allows businesses to use price to market goods. Buying goods in bulk helps to reduce prices below competitor prices.
Promotion	• Small businesses will not necessarily require, nor will they need, expensive advertising and promotions.	• Large businesses can afford to pay for expensive advertising campaigns across all media. • For some this is the most important element in the marketing mix.
Place	• Small businesses generally supply the local market in affordable premises. They will not be able to afford the rents in town centre sites. • Online selling is helping such businesses to sell beyond local markets.	• Large businesses can market their goods virtually anywhere. They can be flexible and easily move out of areas where custom has fallen or costs have risen. • Most have now introduced more online selling and reduced their presence in shopping areas.

Product

A product is any good or service offered for sale to customers.

Product portfolio

REVISED

A new business will often sell one type of product but, as it grows, it will increase the variety of goods and services it provides. This extends the business's **product portfolio** or **product range**. The range may be in similar products (a range of different foods) or in the same area but with different ingredients (a range of different breakfast cereals), or in totally different products (breakfast cereal and stuffed toys). By extending its portfolio a business can:

- sell more and make more profit by satisfying different consumers' wants
- achieve stable sales by:
  - spreading the risks over a variety of products
  - catering for seasonal demand
- achieve sales growth over the range of products.

Product differentiation and USP

REVISED

Product differentiation is used by businesses to make their products stand out from their competitors. By altering the design, features or other aspect of their product, a business can appeal to a variety of market segments and so attract more customers.

One way businesses can attempt to differentiate themselves from their competitors is for each of their products to have a **unique selling point (USP)**. This will be recognised by customers who may be willing to pay a higher price for the product.

Product innovation and design

REVISED

To ensure a wide product portfolio, and that their products are different, businesses work to develop new products and to improve the design of existing products. Before going ahead with a new product, managers will consider other stakeholders.

- **Customers**. Will the new product meet their needs and wants?
- **Competitors**. What products are they producing? Will a new or redesigned product be different enough from the competition?
- **Shareholders**. Will the development costs for a new product or new design be justified with additional profits?

Introducing new products and new designs can be risky.
- The costs of development are high.
- There are no guaranteed sales.

Innovation

Innovation involves:
- Coming up with an idea. This may be the:
  - invention of a new product that solves a consumer problem or issue
  - development of an existing product, perhaps using new technologies
  - adjustment of an existing product, with new colours or flavours.
- Testing the idea to estimate costs and to find out whether there is likely to be a market for the new product.

- Designing the product, perhaps by using Computer Aided Design (CAD). Different designs can be considered.
- Developing the product by building prototypes to find whether the idea works. The product can be researched and tested to find if any problems are likely to emerge.
- Trialling the product by using focus groups and consumer panels.
- Advertising the product to inform customers that the good will be coming onto the market.
- Launching the product onto the market.

> **Product portfolio** or **product range** is the collection or range of goods and services offered by a business.
>
> **Product differentiation** involves distinguishing a product or service from others.
>
> **Innovation** is the process of changing an idea or invention into a good or service for which customers are willing to pay.

Now test yourself

TESTED

1 What is meant by the term product range?
2 What is meant by the term innovation?

Brand

One way for businesses to differentiate their products from those of rivals is by branding. A brand is the name, logo or trademark given to a good or service. Brands are important to businesses for the following reasons:

- They differentiate products from rivals as they are:
  - unique, so rivals cannot use the same brand (it is protected by copyright)
  - associated with business, and can be used on the range of products sold by that business
  - recognised by customers, who will ask for that brand.
- They are used in advertising, and can be recognised by customers at the point of sale. This can lead to impulse buying, which leads to increased sales.
- They encourage brand loyalty. This means customers will continue to buy the product, and other products, with the same brand.
- They enable businesses to charge higher prices.

Not all goods are branded. Some are sold under the brand name of a supermarket chain or other retailer, rather than that of the manufacturer of the product. These are **own brand goods** and are usually cheaper than branded products due to savings made in promotion and packaging costs.

Packaging

An important part of product differentiation and branding is the packaging of the product. Packaging:

- acts as a protection for the goods when:
  - they are transported, to reduce risk of damage
  - they are stored to keep them fresh and clean
- aids storage before sale, by packaging goods in uniform shapes
- allows for easier display on shop shelves
- makes it easier for businesses to brand goods
- enables products to be differentiated from similar products by rivals
- allows customers to recognise the products from advertising or from previous purchase
- means that the customer becomes familiar with the product, so will continue to buy
- enables the business to charge higher prices to cover more than the cost of the packaging, as customers are willing to pay more for more attractive products, for example Easter eggs
- enables the product to stand out on a display, to encourage impulse buying
- ensures that information about the product is available to customers
- allows customers to be aware of use by dates, to reduce health concerns about products.

Packaging can also cause problems for the consumer and society.

- The consumer pays a higher price for goods that have been packaged.
- Consumers can be misled when the packaging hides the true size of the product.
- Many buy too many products in the belief that the product will last longer because of the packaging.
- The packaging may produce environmental issues such as:
  - the use of resources to produce the packaging
  - the litter caused by packaging not being disposed of properly
  - the difficulty in degrading packaging, leading to negative long-term effects on the environment.

Now test yourself

1. What is meant by the term brand?
2. How do own brand goods benefit customers?
3. Outline two ways in which the packaging of food products is good for businesses.
4. What effect does packaging have on the environment?

Product life cycle

Demand for a product or service can change over time. For most products, sales follow a pattern known as the **product life cycle**.

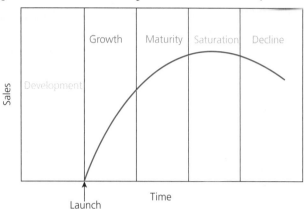

> The **product life cycle** shows how the sales of a product may change over time.

Figure 5.1 A product life cycle

Stages of a product life cycle

Development. This is part of the innovation process.
- **Sales** are zero as the good is being designed and produced before going onto the market.
- **Revenue** is zero as there are no sales.
- **Costs** are high as products are developed, machinery is bought, workers are employed.

Launch or **introduction**. This is when the goods are put on the market for the first time.
- **Sales** are zero or low as customers do not know about the product.
- **Revenue** will be low as promotional pricing encourages buyers.
- **Costs** are high to cover promotional expenditure.

Growth. As more people know of the product demand will increase.
- **Sales** will be rising rapidly as more customers buy the new product.
- **Revenue** will increase with sales and because customers are keen to buy even at higher prices.
- **Costs** are used to pay to produce the goods, but familiarity and word of mouth advertising mean that less advertising is paid for.

Maturity. As more people have the product:
- **Sales** will continue to rise but not at such a rapid rate.
- **Revenue** increases will match the sales.
- **Costs** will continue to be paid to produce the goods.

Saturation. Goods are still being sold but:
- **Sales** will not rise nor fall.
- **Revenue** will be maintained but may start to fall as selling strategies may lead to a fall in price.
- **Costs** may rise as more money is needed to promote the product.

Decline. Fewer sales as customers look for up-to-date alternatives.
- **Sales** fall.
- **Revenue** will also fall as a result.
- **Costs** will be uncertain as the business may cut back on production or it may pay more for marketing.

Now test yourself

1 What is meant by the term product life cycle?
2 Why is the development stage the costliest part of the product life cycle?
3 How will the product life cycle of a bar of chocolate be different from that of clothing?
4 At which point in the product life cycle will sales be neither rising nor falling?

Extension strategies

Businesses might use **extension strategies** to prolong the life cycle of their products. These will be related to marketing mix strategies.

> **Extension strategies** are attempts to maintain the sales of a product and prevent it from entering the decline stage of the product life cycle.

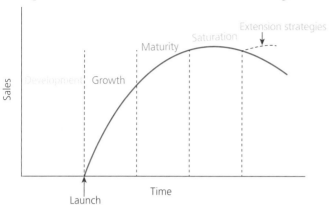

Figure 5.2 Product life cycle extension strategies

Strategies might include:
- Developing new versions of a product with additional features or new flavours in food products. This gives a fresh appeal to the target market.
- Reducing the price permanently or as part of a sales promotion.
- Encouraging customers to buy and use products more frequently.
- Persuading customers to consume products in different seasons.
- Changing the packaging to make it more appealing.
- Entering new markets by trading internationally or appealing to different market segments or selling online.

The product life cycle and business decisions

Businesses will track their sales to estimate where they are on the product life cycle. This will help the managers make decisions about their goods and services. The nature of the product will also help in their considerations about extending the product life cycle. Is it:
- a well-established product? If so, advertising, and making slight changes to recipes, may be enough.
- an entertainment product (such as a film), which may have a short life expectancy? If so, no actions may be necessary as sales decline to zero.
- a fashion product, expected to last one season? The response will be like that for an entertainment product.
- a technological innovation, which will grow and decline when an alternative comes onto the market? If so, the business will be working constantly to invent and innovate new products.

Business decisions may include:
- whether to spend money to develop the product in the first place
- whether investment in buildings and machinery should be made so the good can be produced
- which workers to employ
- how much to spend on the marketing of the launch, and then through the life of the product
- whether to try to extend the life of the product, and so spend money on extension strategies. There needs to be a balance between spending on old products and developing new ones
- when to stop producing the product, with all the costs involved.

Now test yourself

1 What is meant by the term extension strategies?
2 Why might the managers of a business adopt extension strategies?
3 Outline two strategies a business may adopt if the product life cycle is in decline.
4 Suggest two circumstances when businesses will not use extension strategies.

TESTED

Price

Price is part of the marketing mix. Businesses need to set their prices:
- to persuade customers to buy the product to maintain and increase sales. If the price is more than the customer is willing to pay, the customer will not buy.
- to ensure that they at least cover their costs. If the price the producer expects to receive is lower than the amount needed to cover the cost of producing the product and running the business, the goods will not be produced.

Increased sales revenue and paying their costs will lead to higher profits.

The growth of low-price clothes retailers and supermarkets in recent years has shown the importance of price to consumers.

However, some people are still willing to pay high prices for goods because of the importance they feel in owning those goods and because of the belief that the higher the price the better the quality.

Manufacturers and retailers need to use a variety of different tactics or pricing strategies to persuade their customers to buy their goods and services.

> **Cost plus pricing** involves pricing a product by covering the cost of it to the retailer and adding a percentage on top.
>
> **Competitive pricing** is matching the prices that competitors charge.

> **Tip**
>
> Do not assume that the business will always make a profit when using cost plus pricing. The profit per good is only made if that good is sold.

Cost plus pricing　REVISED

Cost plus pricing is a strategy based on the amount of profit the business would like to make rather than on what the market would like to pay.

Benefits	Problems
• Ideal where there is limited price competition between businesses. • Ensures that a profit is made for each good sold.	• Competitor prices may be lower, resulting in poor sales of your product. This could happen if a competitor's costs are low due to, e.g., cheaper rent/labour costs, or utilising economies of scale). • It is not always easy to work out the cost of producing a good. While the variable cost can be straightforward, the contribution of fixed costs to the total cost of a product is more difficult, particularly for large businesses producing a variety of goods.

Competitive pricing　REVISED

Competitive pricing considers what competitors charge, then offers goods at the same or similar prices. If goods are priced higher in one business than others, customers are likely to avoid buying the good at that business, and go elsewhere. This tactic will be used by businesses that sell similar goods to their competitors, such as petrol stations.

Benefit	Problems
• Prices take into consideration the actions of competitors, so customers are less likely to switch to other businesses.	• Costs may be higher in one business than in others: competing on price can lead to lower profits. • Price competition can lead to prices being forced down as businesses compete to gain customers, but there may be no increase in the number of customers. • More advertising may be needed to publicise the price, which increases costs.

Now test yourself
1 Suggest two reasons why price is important to the supplier of goods.
2 What is meant by the term cost plus pricing?
3 Outline two reasons why cost plus pricing may cause problems for businesses.
4 Why is competitive pricing important to (a) customers and (b) businesses?

TESTED

Penetration pricing

Penetration pricing is used when a business charges a very low price for a new product. When the product has become established, the business will increase its price. This strategy is often adopted in highly competitive markets. Some good examples of the types of products that would benefit from the use of penetration pricing are sweets and magazines.

> **Penetration pricing** is launching a new product at a low price to achieve fast sales.

Benefits	Problems
• Lots of people are expected to buy the product at the low price. • It is hoped that a brand loyalty will develop, and that customers will continue to buy even when the price is increased.	• It can be expensive, particularly if the costs of production are not met when the product is first put on the market. • There may be an impression that the product is cheaper than similar goods, so therefore is of a lower quality. • When the price is eventually increased, consumers may refuse to buy the product.

Skimming

Skimming involves setting a high price when the product is new to the market: the price will then be lowered after there have been a few sales at the high price. This strategy introduces products such as technology, or luxury goods for the wealthy to buy – status symbols, that is, an indication of someone's wealth or status.

> **Skimming** is setting a high price for a product when it first enters the market.

Benefits	Problems
• The strategy will result in high profits, even if sales are not high. • It is applied to a specific market segment, so advertising can be directed to that segment. • Prices can be reduced in phases to attract new customers in lower income groups. • Higher sales are generated with each price drop.	• High income earners may not be happy with skimming as, when the price falls, those who are less well-off are able to afford expensive prestige products. • Consumers will be aware that certain businesses have used skimming in the past, so some will delay purchases until the price has fallen.

Psychological pricing

In **psychological pricing**, the business wants its consumers to believe they are gaining a bargain from the purchase of a good. It involves offering goods at prices below a whole number, such as £5.99 or £499. It is hoped that the consumer will believe the product is significantly cheaper than if the price had been £6 or £500.

> **Psychological pricing** occurs when a price is set that has a psychological effect on a consumer's buying decision.

Benefits	Problems
• There are few additional costs in setting up the strategy. • Sales increase as customers are drawn in by the belief that they are obtaining a bargain.	• Many potential customers can see the tactics being adopted and are not influenced by it. • Competitors may follow the pricing strategy, so it has limited effect on sales.

Now test yourself

TESTED

1 What is meant by the term penetration pricing?
2 How does price skimming differ from penetration pricing?
3 What is meant by psychological pricing?
4 Outline one disadvantage for businesses adopting psychological pricing as a strategy.

Loss leaders

Loss leader pricing is a strategy whereby a business sells a product at or below the cost of producing it. This strategy is often used:

- by supermarkets that use products such as bread and milk as their loss leaders. Their loss leaders are heavily advertised so customers are attracted into their store. While at the shop, the customer will buy other goods on which the business earns its profit.
- by businesses that sell a product such as a razor, a printer or a games console at a low price but that sells razor blades, printer ink and console games at high prices. The consumer is drawn in to buy the initial good, then later also buys replacements and add-ons.

> **Loss leaders** involve selling a product at a loss in the hope that the customer will buy other items from the business on which it will make a profit.

Benefits	Problems
• They attract customers into their shops. Subtle repricing of other goods means that little total revenue is lost. • Placing loss leader goods at the rear of a shop encourages customers to browse other stock they pass, leading to purchases not previously considered. • Customers are persuaded into buying other essential products.	• Some customers will be aware of the tactic and will enter the shop just for the loss leader item. • Loss leaders cannot be used for all goods. They are mainly used for essential goods that are bought regularly.

Price discrimination

Price discrimination is a strategy in which businesses charge different prices to different customers for the same product. Discrimination pricing can be based on factors such as where people live, their ages and when they can travel. This strategy is mainly found in service industries.

> **Price discrimination** is when a business charges different prices for the same service or good.

Benefits	Problems
• The strategy is based on the ability of the segment to pay for products. • Businesses can maximise their sales in different sectors.	• Some customers may be resentful that others are paying lower prices. • Businesses may need to set up ways to ensure that customers in one segment do not pay the lower prices available to others in a different segment.

> **Tip**
>
> Not all strategies apply to all goods and circumstances. Read the question carefully to ensure that any suggested strategies are relevant to the question.

Factors influencing price and pricing strategies

The choice to use a particular pricing strategy is business and context specific, and many different factors influence a product's price. Key factors include:

- The cost of producing the goods and services.
- The demand for the product and customer's willingness to pay the price.
- The competitive nature of the market regarding:
  - the prices other businesses charge
  - the quality of their goods and services.
- The objectives of the business and whether the business wants to increase market share or maximise profits.
- Where the product is in its life cycle. At launch and decline prices may need to be low but at maturity they could be at their highest.
- The relationship with the rest of the marketing mix. Is the quality of the product more important than its price?

> **Now test yourself**
>
> 1 Outline two occasions when loss leaders may be used as a pricing strategy.
> 2 What is meant by the term price discrimination?
>
> TESTED

Promotion

Promotional methods used by business

REVISED

The **promotional** methods used by businesses include the following, which will be examined in more detail below:

- advertising
- sales promotion
- direct marketing.

Advertising

REVISED

Businesses have a range of **advertising media** that will be paid for to provide information and to persuade consumers to buy their products.

> **Promotion** involves information and techniques used by businesses to make consumers aware of products and to persuade them to buy those products now and in the future.
>
> **Advertising media** are the various places where advertisements may be found.

Printed media

Local and national press

This involves using newspapers, magazines and journals.

Benefits	Problems
<ul><li>Tends to be cheaper than other media, particularly local newspapers.</li><li>May be kept for some time, which can re-remind readers of product details.</li><li>Much information can be provided in the media, e.g. sizes and prices of products, retailers, contact details of the business.</li><li>The advertising can be placed in sections of the newspaper to appeal to certain market segments.</li><li>The advertisements may be in colour, so they are more easily seen, recognised and remembered.</li><li>The printed advertisements can include promotions such as money-off coupons and competitions.</li><li>Local newspapers can be directed at local markets, so money is not wasted on markets where the products may not be available.</li></ul>	<ul><li>Small readerships that are decreasing as more people obtain news online.</li><li>The quality of colour printing in newspapers may not be good.</li><li>A limited display with no sound nor movement.</li><li>Advertisements do not to stand out and may be missed or ignored.</li><li>Advertisements may be lost among the other advertisements in a newspaper.</li><li>Advertisements of some products (such as alcohol and tobacco) are banned in some countries.</li></ul>

Leaflets and flyers

These can be handed out to the public or distributed to their homes.

Benefits	Problems
● Can be kept for reference by consumers. ● Can be handed to possible customers in selected market segments. ● Can include detailed information. ● Colour may be used to attract customers.	● May be thrown away, unlooked at, by disinterested individuals, resulting in few new customers. ● The average cost of producing the leaflets may be high.

Directory listings

These give an alphabetic list of the contact details of businesses usually set out according to the type of business. Listing may be free, but businesses can pay for enlarged entries and advertisements, so their details stand out.

Benefits	Problems
● Directories are often kept in households for a long time. ● Each entry is targeted towards customers wishing to buy a certain good or service. ● Directories are available for shoppers 24 hours a day, so can be referred to when needed. ● Responses to advertisements can be tracked by advertisers using special telephone numbers, so the effectiveness of the advertising can be measured.	● Advertisements can be expensive for the area covered by the directory. ● Directories are usually published once a year, so advertisers will have one chance to write an effective advertisement and will have to wait to change them for future editions. ● Online directories and search engines have reduced the need for printed directories.

Now test yourself

TESTED ☐

1 What is meant by the term advertising media?
2 Suggest one reason why a business might use flyers to advertise its products.
3 Outline one advantage for businesses that newspaper advertising has over the use of flyers.
4 What is an advantage of using directories as a means of promoting a business?

> **Tip**
>
> In answering questions about advertising media, avoid using words such as 'cheap' without developing the word, by suggesting why the medium is cheap or by comparing it with another medium.

Broadcast and other media

Radio

Radio can broadcast advertisements into people's homes, cars and workplaces.

Benefits	Problems
● Radio advertisements are cheap to produce. ● They can offer a wide coverage when used nationally. ● Can appeal to nearby markets when used locally. ● Advertisements can appeal to specific markets when used in special interest broadcasts. ● Advertisements can use a range of methods to appeal to consumers, such as music and humour.	● Radio is often used as a background for listeners, so advertisements may be missed. ● Customers do not have a written record, so product details may be misheard or overlooked.

Television

Television has been the main medium used for many years although it has faced greater competition with the growth of the internet.

Benefits	Problems
● Television has a vast coverage, as most homes have a television. ● Advertisements attract an audience's attention through movement, music, colour, humour and demonstrations of the product. ● Advertisements can appeal to specific market segments when used in special interest broadcasts, and at the times of day when certain markets are likely to be watching. ● Advertisements are often repeated to reinforce the message for customers.	● Television advertising is very expensive. ● Mainly suitable for mass market products. ● Advertisements are short, so an immediate impact is needed for consumers to remember the message. ● Advertisements of some products (such as alcohol and tobacco) are banned in some countries. ● There is a time lag between seeing the advertisement and having the opportunity to buy the product. ● Improvements in technology mean that possible customers can avoid television advertising.

Cinema

Increased popularity of cinemas makes the medium attractive to advertisers.

Benefits	Problems
● It is difficult for watchers to avoid the advertisements. ● The quality of the sound and the size of the screen allows for greater impact. ● Television advertisements can be shown at cinemas to reinforce the advertisements watched at home. ● Showing advertisements in cinemas is cheaper than showing them on television, so local businesses can afford to advertise. ● The advertisements can be targeted at a market segment according to the film being shown.	● Unless the customer is a regular cinema goer, it is difficult to reinforce the message. ● The size of the cinema will restrict the number of people who see the advertisement.

Point of sale

Many manufacturers will provide display materials and signs for use in shops. Some retailers will advertise and display goods close to the tills. Both are examples of advertising at the point of sale.

Benefits	Problems
● Customers may be tempted to buy goods on impulse. ● Displays can be changed quickly.	● The displays may restrict space in shops and at the tills. ● Only a limited range of goods can be displayed.

Online

The internet and online world is another very effective media avenue for advertising. This is reviewed in more detail in the following section.

Now test yourself

TESTED

1 Give two reasons why a sole trader may advertise on a local radio station.
2 Outline two reasons why there are few small businesses advertising on national television.
3 How do businesses benefit from advertising in cinemas?
4 What is point of sale advertising?

Technology and advertising

The development of the internet and other electronic technologies has greatly added to the ways businesses can promote and advertise their products. This has involved the use of the following:

- **Social media**
  Businesses have begun using **social media** websites and applications, such as twitter, Facebook and Instagram, to create links between their products and potential customers. They can also follow the reaction of other social media users to their products. This is a cheap method of advertising and promotion for businesses, although specialised workers may need to be employed to post updated social media content, and to monitor social media reactions to the businesses products (and those of their competitors).

- **Blogs**
  Blogs are similar to social media websites, but generally with fewer content space restrictions. Businesses can provide more detailed outlines of the goods and services they produce, along with video demonstrations of products.

- **Search engine advertising**
  Search engines, such as Google or Bing, are generally free to the user. Instead, the search engine will charge businesses a fee to ensure their products appear at the top of search results, or for clearly visible adverts. Both methods aim to attract the attention of the individual carrying out the search.

- **Pop-up adverts**
  Technology means that unrequested advertisements can appear on computer browser windows. Other technologies can be used by computer users to block these.

- **Digital adverting**
  Digital displays extend the use of posters on billboard sites and at sporting venues. The displays can be changed easily between advertisers and can show movement. They are particularly valuable to advertisers in busy locations and to those advertising at televised sporting events.

- **Mobile advertising**
  Mobile advertising is a method of advertising used on smart phones and tablets. Businesses use text messages, downloaded applications or mobile games to advertise their products.

Social media involves websites and applications that allow users to create and share information, ideas and interests with other individuals, communities and networks.

Blogs provide information and allow discussion on the internet with other users producing their own entries or posts.

Search engine advertising is a form of online marketing that places advertisements on web pages showing the results from search engine queries.

Pop-up adverts are a form of online marketing that place new browser windows on computer screens.

Evaluation of online advertising

Benefits	Problems
• It is available to markets across the world. • Advertisements can be viewed and responded to at any time. • It is interactive between business and customer so that questions can be asked and answered immediately. • Advertisements can be targeted at appropriate market segments. • Advertisements can be changed quickly so that sales promotions can be offered at short notice. • The number of responses to the advertisements can be monitored. • It is relatively cheap, once websites have been designed. • Advertisements can result in immediate purchases. • Consumers are given detailed information about products.	• Technical problems may arise when displaying and ordering products. • Coverage may be restricted to those who can use the internet. • Advertising on the internet is highly competitive and it may be difficult for small businesses to be noticed on search engines. • The use of pop-ups and so on may make the sites difficult to navigate and may put off customers. • Websites may be expensive to construct.

Now test yourself

TESTED ☐

1 What is meant by the term social media?
2 How can businesses use blogs to market their products?
3 Who pays the cost of search engine advertising?
4 Outline one benefit for businesses using digital advertising.

Sales promotion

REVISED ☐

A sales promotion is a short-term measure attempting to encourage customers to buy products. Methods include:

● **Promotional pricing**. This involves discounts or price reductions during sales periods to promote products.
● **Special offers** such as 'buy one get one free' (or BOGOF). This encourages customers to buy more than they had intended.
● Competitions offering **prizes** to customers who submit slogans. These require customers to include labels from products with their entries so sales increase.
● **Coupons** are given when a sale is made, which give reductions on future purchases, encouraging customers to return.
● **Point of sale** displays are found near the tills. They attract the attention of customers who may be tempted to buy items spontaneously.
● **Free gifts** may be given to customers who buy items. They may be included with the products or obtained by sending proof of purchase to the manufacturer.
● **Free samples** and testers often encourage customers to buy the good if they like the sample.

Evaluation of sales promotion

Benefits	Problems

• They attract more customers who:
  – may be new to the market
  – may be persuaded away from competitors.
• They can be used at any time during the life of the product.
• They can often be used alongside advertising.
	• They cannot stand alone, and must be used with other aspects of marketing.
	• They are short lived.
	• Brand image may be affected if used too often.
	• They are expensive and may lead to a rise in price of the product.

Direct marketing

REVISED

Many businesses will attempt to market their goods directly to customers. They can build up a database of information about individuals, groups and communities through loyalty cards, internet search histories and area sales records. Customers are then contacted through the post, telephone calls, pop-up advertising on web browsers and emails.

Evaluation of direct marketing

Benefits	Problems
● Customers for particular goods can be targeted. ● The marketing can include the names of customers so they believe it is just for them. ● The success or failure of the marketing can be easy to measure by counting the responses. ● Databases are fairly cheap to manage.	● Response rates can be low so the cost per successful contact may be high. ● Customers often do not like contacts that are considered to be junk mail or spam in their emails. ● It is difficult to ensure the accuracy of databases.

Factors influencing the promotional activities

REVISED

Businesses can choose to use a mix of sales promotion methods. The methods used will depend on:
● The cost of the promotion and the finance available. Special offers may be expensive but point of sale display may be cheaper.
● The nature of the target market. Wealthier customers may be more influenced by some promotional methods than poorer customers.
● The activities of competitors. Businesses will sometimes match the promotions of competitors.
● The type of market. Businesses in a large market will be wealthy enough to carry out wide-reaching sales promotions. Local businesses will only be able to afford low level promotions.
● The type of product. Businesses producing expensive consumer durable goods are more likely to use point of sale displays and gifts than special offers.

Now test yourself

TESTED

1 What is meant by the term discount?
2 Suggest how competitions may improve the sale of products.
3 Describe two forms of sales promotion that a flower shop could use.
4 What is direct marketing?

Place

Place is where buyers and sellers meet. The buyer spends money and the seller exchanges goods and services. Place could include shops, markets, telephone sales, the internet and so on. Goods are produced by manufacturers and are bought by customers. To enable this process to happen efficiently, other businesses usually come between the manufacturer and the customer. These are known as **intermediaries**. Together they form the **channel of distribution**.

Product distribution channels

REVISED

Distribution channels usually involve:
- **Manufacturers**. These are the people who produce the good or service.
- **Wholesalers**. These buy large quantities of product, or **bulk**, which they then break into smaller amounts to sell, so the **wholesalers break bulk**. Wholesalers have other functions such as:
  - selling the products of many manufacturers, who do not themselves have to negotiate with individual **retailers**, thereby keeping costs down
  - storing goods in their warehouses
  - displaying goods for retailers to select
  - offering advice to retailers
  - providing trade credit and transporting goods to the retailer.
- **Retailers**. These are at the end of the channel of distribution.

The main channels of distribution are:
- **Manufacturer → Wholesaler → Retailer → Consumer**
  The manufacturer sells to wholesalers who distribute goods to local retailers. Customer prices may be higher as each intermediary will expect a profit but savings in distribution costs may offset this.
- **Manufacturer → Retailer → Consumer**
  The manufacturer supplies directly to the retailer. It is used when:
  - The retailer operates on a large scale and can afford to carry out the functions of the wholesaler by buying directly from the manufacturer. The savings can be passed on to the consumer.
  - The products are bulky such as furniture or cars, so are more easily sent directly to the retailer. Fewer costs need to be passed on to customers so prices are generally lower than they would otherwise be.
  - The products may be perishable and should be distributed quickly.
- **Manufacturer → Consumer**
  The product is sold directly to the customer. This method is often used:
  - for products made using job production
  - when firms selling technological goods sell directly to customers
  - when some businesses, which have traditionally sold their products door to door, continue the practice and now sell through their websites.

Prices may be lower as intermediary profits will not be paid but the nature of the products and distribution costs may lead to high prices being paid.

Place is where the product is available for the consumer to purchase.

The **channel of distribution** describes how the ownership of a product passes from the producer to the final customer.

Wholesalers buy in large quantities from a producer and sell to retailers in smaller quantities.

Retailers sell directly to the customer.

Benefits	Problems
• Producers can reach more consumers by selling to wholesalers and retailers who are closer to the customers, so they save the cost of distribution. • Consumers have goods available locally, so there is no need to travel to manufacturers. • The above may have environmental benefits, with goods being available close to consumers.	• Wholesalers and retailers want their own profits: goods may be more expensive than if they are sold directly to customers by manufacturers. • Once the good is sold by manufacturers, they have less control over the marketing of their products.

Now test yourself

TESTED

1 What is an intermediary?
2 Outline two differences between wholesalers and retailers.

The increasing importance of e-commerce and m-commerce `REVISED`

Customers have taken advantage of developments in technology and the growth of retailer websites to change how goods are bought. Customers:
- do not need to travel to buy goods and services
- can shop at any time
- can buy goods directly from businesses around the world.

Therefore, e-commerce and m-commerce have become more important. The use of e- and m- technology was examined on page 26.

Effects on physical retail outlets

Retail businesses and stakeholders have been affected by the growth of e-commerce.

- Several large retailers now concentrate sales in fewer outlets.
- Supermarket businesses have put off plans to build out-of-town shops as shopping habits have changed and even food products are bought online.
- Local communities have lost their well-known branded shops as well as smaller shops.
- Employees in local shops have lost their jobs as the work moves elsewhere.
- Retail businesses have moved to compete with the providers of e-commerce with the development of **multi-channel distribution**.

Multi-channel distribution involves a business using more than one route to distribute its goods.

Multi-channel distribution `REVISED`

Tip

Do not confuse multi-channel distribution with multinational companies. Read the question carefully.

Multi-channel distribution offers customers a choice of ways to buy.
- **In store**, where customers can view the product and compare it with similar products.
- **On business websites**, where detailed descriptions are provided and photographs shown. Goods can be paid for and delivered to the customer's home or to the store.
- **With the help of comparison websites**, on which the products and prices of different suppliers can be compared. Some of these favour certain brands or outlets.

- **Telephone sales**, which enable customers with limited internet ability to order products having seen these in shops or online.
- **Printed catalogues**, which enable customers to compare products before ordering online, by mail order or by telephone.

By providing a variety of methods to sell goods, businesses are more able to:
- **compete with rivals** who may be using a range of methods
- **maximise sales** by widening the market beyond high streets
- **maximise profits** by closing expensive, surplus stores
- **provide customers with the choice** on how they buy products and the convenience to do so when it is most convenient
- **gain customer loyalty**.

Getting the right channel of distribution `REVISED`

Whichever channel of distribution a business chooses, its main aim is to make a profit. To do this sales and revenue need to be as high as possible and costs as low as possible. The right channel will ensure that:
- goods are available where the customer wants them and when the customer needs them so that sales can be maximised.
- goods are distributed as cheaply as possible through intermediaries or from shops or warehouses. The wrong decision will mean prices are too high and the goods will not be sold.

Now test yourself `TESTED`

1 What is e-commerce?
2 Outline the difference between e-commerce and m-commerce.
3 How does e-commerce help businesses to keep their costs down?
4 Why do many businesses still sell goods in shopping centres?

6 Human resources

Recruitment

 REVISED

Businesses often need to employ new workers. This will be necessary when:
- sales rise
- workers retire or leave for jobs elsewhere
- new goods and services are being produced.

It is important that businesses have processes to select employees because:
- They aim to provide quality goods and services to satisfy customers and increase sales.
- They need to maximise the **productivity** or output of each employee. This will help the businesses to keep costs down and earn profits.
- They need to keep workers for as long as possible. Recruiting suitable workers means they should stay for longer. This is important because:
  - It is expensive to recruit replacement workers because of the costs of advertising, the money and time used by workers to carry out the recruitment process, and the cost of training the new workers.
  - New workers will not be as skilful as workers who have left.
  - New workers will not produce as many goods as those who have left.

Possible employees will need to go through a recruitment process to ensure that they have the best combination of:
- **skills**, so that training for the new workers can be minimised
- **training**, so that training costs for the new workers can be kept low
- **qualifications**, which may be general, to show a good all-round education, or specific to the job
- **experience** in relevant work to show that the person has done similar work before, or general experience of the work environment
- **personality**, with such qualities as being hard working, being able to get on with others, leadership skills and so on.

When recruiting workers businesses may consider several methods including:
- **Internal recruitment**.

> **Internal recruitment** takes place when a job vacancy is filled from within the existing workforce.
>
> **External recruitment** is filling a job vacancy with any suitable person not already employed by the business.

Benefits	Problems
• Advertising and training costs are low. • Worker motivation may be increased as employees aim for promotion.	• The most talented people may not be available internally. • New ideas are not brought into the business. • Some workers may resent not getting promoted.

- **External recruitment**.

Benefits	Problems
• More talented workers than those within the business may be available. • New skills, talents and ideas may be brought into the business.	• Advertising will be expensive. • There may be some resentment from existing workers who believe that promotion should be internal.

Now test yourself

1 Why will businesses need to recruit workers?
2 How do businesses gain from recruiting externally?

TESTED ✓

The recruitment process

The recruitment process is a standardised way of identifying and selecting potential new employees, however the methods of recruitment can vary. Both process and methods are looked at in detail now.

Preparing for selection

Once a business has **identified a job vacancy** and decided to recruit new workers it will:

- prepare a **job description**. This shows what the job is about including:
  - ○ the job title
  - ○ the type of work
  - ○ duties and responsibilities of the job
  - ○ who the worker will be responsible to and who the worker is responsible for
  - ○ wage or salary information
  - ○ the work time, including holidays
  - ○ location of the work.
- prepare a **person specification**, which includes:
  - ○ the qualifications, academic and vocational, of the person applying
  - ○ the relevant experience of the applicant
  - ○ any additional skills of the applicant
  - ○ the type of person required, including personality and interests.
- **advertise** the job including details from the job description and person specification. This can be done internally, for example by company magazines or on works' noticeboards. This is a cheap means of advertising, but the number of candidates, and their range of skills, may be limited.

  Or externally, which involves looking outside of the business, for example through the following channels:
  - ○ Newspapers and magazines. These could be national or local depending on the importance of the job and the demand for workers in the local area or further afield. This attracts applicants from a much wider area, but newspaper advertising can be expensive.
  - ○ Online. These could attract applicants from across the world.
  - ○ Recruitment agencies. These are experts in recruitment and have many contacts, but they are expensive and will not be suitable for finding workers for low skilled jobs.
  - ○ Jobcentre Plus branches. These are run by the Government to link businesses with unemployed workers.

People who are interested in advertised jobs will apply for them using some, or all, of the following:

- **application form**, where personal details, qualifications, experience and interests are included. Contact details for people willing to support the application will also be included.
- letter of application, where reasons for applying for the job can be explained.
- **curriculum vitae (CV)**, which includes all the details found in an application form and will be sent when no form is available.
- **informal contact**, which may be made by telephone, letter or a visit to the business when the applicant is looking for a job that might have been recommended by a friend. For lower level jobs the employer may be so impressed as to offer a job without going through the rest of the recruitment process.

A **job description** states information about the duties and tasks that make up a job.

A **person specification** sets out the qualifications and skills required by an employee to fill a job.

Tip

Be certain that you know the difference between a job description and a person specification.

Now test yourself

1 What is a job description?
2 How is a person specification different from a job description?
3 Where is a business likely to advertise if it wants to recruit from around the world?
4 What is a CV?

TESTED

Making the selection

- **Shortlist**. The business will use the person specification to draw up a list of people who have applied for the job and who appear to have the right abilities and qualities for the job. This is called **shortlisting**.
- **References** are provided by people chosen by the person applying for a job to support the application. **References** may be provided by:
  - previous employers who comment on the person's working abilities and their attendance and punctuality
  - schools and colleges who comment on the applicant's work, the way they get on with others and their involvement in school activities
  - others who know the person such as friends or work colleagues who comment on personal skills or general interests.
- **Interview**. This is an opportunity for the business to find out more about the applicants and for the applicant to impress the managers of the business. Depending on the job and the size of the business interviews can be carried out:
  - **face to face** between the applicant and a group of interviewers
  - **by telephone**. This may be used to save the travel costs of an interview or for less important jobs
  - **online**. This saves travel costs.

Interviews are a long-established method used during the selection process and they generally lead to the appointment of the right workers. However, sometimes the wrong individual can be selected. This may be because:

- Some people perform badly at interview, perhaps because of nerves or lack of interview practice, but they may have the best abilities and skills.
- Some interviewers are not so skilled in asking the right questions or their selection may be based on the appearance of the people being interviewed.

Businesses have therefore introduced other processes such as:

- **skills tests**, which find whether the applicant has numerical or practical skills. Such tests can be carried out online.
- **aptitude tests**, which find whether the applicant can apply the skills to situations.
- **group tests**, which put the applicants in teams who are then set a relevant problem to solve. The applicants are watched to find their teamwork, leadership and practical skills.
- **roleplay**, which puts the applicant in an imaginary situation, relevant to the job, to observe how they respond.
- **psychometric tests**, which are multiple choice tests that can help to show the personality of candidates for jobs.

The results of these tests can help the managers in the selection process to decide which of the applicants has the right abilities, skills and personality for the job and which is most likely to be suitable for that business and job.

- **Selection and appointment**. After the interviews and tests are completed, the managers select the best person. References are often checked at this stage. If everything is satisfactory, the individual can be offered the job.

> **Shortlisting** is the process of selecting the most suitable applicants from those people who apply for a job.
>
> **References** are statements of an applicant's suitability for a job.

Recruitment in different situations

All businesses will use their own systems when recruiting workers. The size of the business will sometimes determine how businesses recruit workers.

	Large businesses	Small businesses
Person specification and job description	The size of the organisation means that everyone involved in recruitment will need to know the jobs to be done and the type of person required. Formal descriptions are needed.	The owners of the business will know the job to be done and the type of person needed so less formal descriptions are needed. However, the applicants will need to know what the job entails and whether they have the requirements to be able to do the job.
Applying for the job	Large businesses have formal processes and may expect many applicants. They will tend to produce application forms and/or require letters of application and CVs.	Fewer applications will be expected so letters and CVs will be acceptable. Some will allow applicants to apply by telephone.
Shortlist	This will generally be drawn up.	Often not necessary because of the small number of applicants.
References	Formal written references will be required to be used at the interview and to help with selection although some will only be requested after selection, before the confirmation that a person is being offered the job.	Written references are often required but sometimes less formal telephone references will be used.
Interview	Large firms have the resources to hold face-to-face formal interviews with applicants and managers.	The small number of applicants means that interviews can be less formal and may be carried out over the telephone.
Tests	Large businesses have the resources to use tests as part of the selection process.	Small businesses will probably not be able to afford these.
Selection	Consultations between managers and the need to wait for references mean that applicants will need to wait before being informed about success or otherwise.	Often successful and unsuccessful applicants can be told immediately.

Now test yourself

TESTED

1 Why is a shortlist drawn up?
2 Who would a school leaver be likely to ask for a reference?
3 What benefits do interviews have when recruiting workers?
4 Why might businesses use methods other than interviews in the recruitment process?

Training

The benefits of training

Every year businesses spend large sums of money on **training** to improve the skills and knowledge of their workers. Training:

- **improves productivity**. As workers improve their knowledge and skills they produce more goods, at a faster rate, with fewer mistakes.
- **improves worker morale**. As more skills are learned, workers feel better about their abilities and are more motivated to work.
- **improves products**. Workers can produce better quality goods so there will be fewer errors in production and customers may be willing to pay more for higher quality goods.
- **improves services**. As more skills are learned, this helps to …

- **improve customer satisfaction**, so businesses do not have to spend large sums of money in response to customer complaints, and …
- **reduce wastage** as goods are not rejected during quality control.
- helps businesses **stay ahead of the competition**, as customers are aware of the quality and become loyal to the business.
- helps to **reduce costs** with:
  - a more contented workforce remaining with the business, so recruitment costs are kept as low as possible.
  - the reduction in wastage of materials or finished products.

When is training needed?

Workers need to be trained for a number of reasons.

Induction training

Induction training is used when workers are first employed so that they become familiar with their new surroundings and the specific methods and policies of the business. It may be as basic as the location of toilets and the canteen, through to the workings of the work's IT systems or to employment practices, responsibilities, and health and safety issues.

Retraining

Retraining happens when an employee has been working for the business for some time in cases where:

- the worker has not been working to the required standard and skills need to be refreshed. Retraining is cheaper than dismissing a worker and recruiting a replacement.
- the roles and responsibilities of the worker have changed so new skills need to be taught.

New technology

Advances in technology mean that skills must be updated.

New health and safety requirements

Workers need to be trained to ensure a safe working environment.

Creating opportunities for employees

As workers become more experienced in the workplace, they may increase their duties and responsibilities. Training will be needed to allow them to take the opportunities. Promotion and extra pay may follow.

> **Training** is a range of activities giving employees job-related skills and knowledge.
>
> **Induction training** is the training given to employees when they first start a job.

Now test yourself

1 How do (a) businesses and (b) workers benefit from training?
2 Why is induction training needed?
3 Why Is it necessary to train workers who have been with a business for some time?
4 How do technological developments affect training?

Types of training

On-the-job training

In **on-the-job training**, workers learn from more experienced colleagues via demonstrations, **coaching**, **mentoring**, **job shadowing** and **job rotation**:

- **Demonstrations**, where the worker is shown how to perform specific tasks using appropriate skills.
- **Coaching** by a worker's line manager who teaches specific skills and sets goals for improvement.
- **Mentoring** involves a senior employee advising and guiding the junior.
- **Job shadowing**, where the trainee follows other workers to understand the full role of the job. Workers may also offer advice and guidance.
- **Job rotation** involves workers moving to different areas of production to learn skills and responsibilities across the workplace.

> **On-the-job training** is given in the workplace.
>
> **Coaching** involves an experienced employee providing guidance and support to a less experienced worker.
>
> **Mentoring** is a training system whereby a senior and experienced employee provides training to a more junior worker.

Benefits	Problems

• Cheap, as the trainee works alongside experienced workers.
• Quick to organise within the workplace, and given when needed.
• Effective and relevant as the trainee is supervised by other workers.
	• It may not provide the right training as:
	  – It depends on the skills of other workers, who may have a narrow knowledge of what is required.
	  – The trainer may have poor communication skills.
	  – The trainer may pass on bad work practices to the trainee.
	• The time the trainer spends with the trainee is time they could have spent on their own tasks, meaning a fall in productivity.

Off-the-job training

Off-the-job training is provided by people and organisations not employed by the business. It includes:

- **off-site** training at further education colleges and universities. The employee can gain vocational qualifications and perhaps a degree.
- **computer based** training with programs developing general skills produced by external businesses.
- **sandwich courses**, where employees study for qualifications on a part-time basis, or a for a degree that includes a period of time in the middle of the course spent working for the business.
- **use of outside trainers**. Specialist training companies offer courses such as the use of IT or health and safety issues. These are held in the workers' own offices.

> **Job shadowing** is a form of training whereby experienced employees are followed throughout the working day by trainees.
>
> **Job rotation** is the regular switching of staff between jobs of a similar degree of complexity.
>
> **Off-the-job training** is provided outside the employee's place of work.

Benefits	Problems
• A wide range of up-to-date skills gained. • Skills can be taught by experienced trainers with a professional, high quality approach. • Workers can gain qualifications, which will improve their morale and their work. • Workers feel motivated as the business is spending money on their training.	• Training will be expensive as professional trainers will be employed. • Workers are often trained away from the business, so they will not be producing goods and services. • As a variety of skills are taught, training may not be aimed at specific needs of the firm. • Qualifications gained by the workers may be of value to competitors, which may lead to workers leaving as they have a higher value in the job market.

Now test yourself

1 What is meant by on-the-job training?
2 Why is off-the-job training likely to be more expensive than on-the-job training?

Motivation

Note

There is no need to know motivational theories.

Motivation is about wanting to work every day and wanting to do as well as possible while in work. This motivation comes from the workers' desire to do well for themselves and for the business, and the ways the business acts to encourage employees to work hard and efficiently.

The benefits of a motivated workforce

REVISED

Lower levels of absenteeism

Well-motivated workers want to be at work and are less likely to take time off without good cause. High levels of **absenteeism** will affect businesses, for example:

- They will still have to pay the worker, as well as any replacement.
- The replacement will not know the job as well as the absentee employee, so the work is not done as efficiently.
- The quality of goods and services may not be as high.

Retention of workers

Motivated workers will want to remain in their job, so there will be low levels of staff turnover. This benefits the business as it will not have the costs of recruiting and training replacement workers.

Improved relations between management and workers

When workers are well motivated, they will get on with management. This means that:

- Workers will be less resistant to change.
- There will be fewer industrial disputes involving trade unions.
- The business will have a better reputation as an employer, and so find it easier to recruit workers if necessary.

More innovation and creativity

Workers may be inspired to improve their working methods and suggest improvements.

Improved worker performance

Motivated workers work hard and do their jobs as well as possible. They:

- arrive at work on time
- use their time at work effectively

- will produce a larger quantity of goods or services so the business can employer fewer workers so
  - goods can be produced more cheaply and
  - labour costs for producing each good will be lower so
  - goods can be produced at lower prices so the business is more competitive.

Improved quality and customer service

Motivated workers want to maintain the quality of the goods they produce and the services they provide. This is helped by the skills and experience of workers who remain with the business for a long time.

A better reputation

Suppliers and customers will act more favourably when they see a better motivated workforce. This will also apply to future employees, so it will be easier to recruit better workers.

Higher profits

The above benefits will help the business to promote sales and to reduce costs and so be able to increase profits.

Absenteeism occurs when an employee is not present at work.

Now test yourself

TESTED

1. Why are well-motivated workers less likely to be absent from work?
2. Why is it likely to be more expensive for businesses with high levels of worker turnover?
3. How do good relations between workers and managers help growing businesses?
4. What effects will a well-motivated workforce have on the output of businesses?

Methods used to motivate workers

Financial methods

Businesses use money to pay, reward and motivate their workers.

Wages

Wages are generally paid to shop and factory workers and are based on either time rates or **piece rates**:

- **Time rates**. An hourly rate is agreed and wages are paid weekly or monthly according to the number of hours worked. If more than the agreed number of hours have been worked, employees may be paid at a higher rate for the extra hours, which are called **overtime**.
- **Piece rates**. Wages are paid according to the number of goods a worker has produced.

Whether workers are paid time rates or piece rates or a combination of the two, employers must make certain that they pay a fair wage. This is decided by the Government, which says that all workers must be paid a **National Living Wage**.

Salaries

Salaries are paid to workers in management and professional positions. This is an annual amount, based on an employee's work for the year and is usually paid monthly.

Workers will be motivated with the payment of higher wages and salaries.

Performance-related pay

This is an additional payment to workers who reach management-set targets. Such pay may involve:

- **Commission**, paid to sales staff based on the number of goods sold, so they will be motivated to sell more.
- **Bonuses**, paid when non-sales staff exceed what is required of them in production or dealing with customers. The harder they work, the higher the bonuses.

Profit sharing

This is paid to workers when profits are made by the business. All employees are motivated to increase profits, as they will receive a share of these.

Financial fringe benefits

Fringe benefits are rewards above wages and salaries, and can include:

- **staff discounts**, for those who buy products from employers
- **company cars**, used for work but available for private use
- **health insurance**, which benefits employees and their families and the business by helping sick employees to return to work.

These rewards motivate employees and keep them loyal to the business as they do not want to lose the benefits.

Piece rate is a method of payment under which employees are paid according to the quantity of products they produce.

Overtime is a higher hourly rate that is paid to employees for any additional hours worked.

The **National Living Wage** is an hourly rate of pay that is set by the Government. All employees above a certain age must receive at least this rate of pay.

Commission is a payment to an employee based on achieving a certain level of sales.

A **bonus** is an additional payment to an employee for achieving an agreed target.

Fringe benefits are the extras employees may receive in addition to their pay.

Non-financial methods

Money need not be the only way to motivate workers. Other methods include:

Job enlargement

With **job enlargement**, workers are given additional tasks to reduce the monotony of the workplace and to motivate them.

Job rotation

With job rotation, workers take on different jobs within the business for a set time. This reduces boredom and helps employees to appreciate the work done elsewhere.

Job enrichment

With **job enrichment**, workers are given more complicated, responsible tasks in addition to the work they already do.

Empowerment

Empowerment allows workers more control over how they do their work. They make their own decisions with little supervision. Workers are motivated to do their best within their part of the business for the benefit of all.

Training

For the above to succeed training is needed in new skills. As well as improving their skills, training increases workers' confidence and motivation.

Motivation in different situations

Large businesses will have the financial resources and the number of workers to be able to use the full range of motivational methods available. Smaller businesses will tend to rely on financial rewards to encourage their employees. However, the closeness of workers and owners in small businesses will mean that employees are encouraged by a more personal approach to motivation. Also, the size of the business means that tasks will need to be shared so methods close to job enlargement, job enrichment and empowerment are used automatically in the working environment.

> **Job enlargement** is redesigning a worker's job so that it contains more tasks of a similar level of difficulty.
>
> **Job enrichment** is designing a job to give interesting and challenging tasks.
>
> **Empowerment** gives employees greater control over their working lives.

Now test yourself

TESTED

1 If a business receives an urgent order, how can it use time rates to complete the order?
2 How are fringe benefits of value for businesses that want to keep their workers?
3 Explain which non-financial method gives workers experience of more of the business.
4 How does empowerment (a) motivate the worker and (b) benefit the business?

Organisational structures

Regardless of their size, businesses need to organise their workforce to be as efficient as possible. With small businesses, this is straightforward as owners give instructions to workers. As the business grows, this becomes more complicated.

Within businesses there are several roles and responsibilities.

> An **organisational structure** is the way a business arranges itself to carry out its activities.

Roles and responsibilities within a business

Owners and leaders

With sole traders and partnerships, the owners will be the leaders. This is also the case for the majority shareholder in small private limited companies. Public limited companies tend to be so large that the owners – the shareholders – pass responsibility for leadership to a Board of Directors. Among these will be the managing director who will have control over the day-to-day leadership.

The owners and leaders:
- set the aims and objectives
- set the targets to achieve these
- monitor whether the targets are being met.

Characteristics of owners and leaders

- **Authority**. They have most **authority** and power over the workforce.
- **Decision making**. They make the medium- and long-term decisions about the business and set overall targets for the business.
- **Skills and qualities**. They will have had the time inside and outside the business to gain the qualifications and experience to carry out their roles.
- **Delegation**. Some of their responsibilities and authority will be passed down (**delegated**) to managers.
- **Pay and benefits**. They will have the highest salaries, with bonuses for meeting targets.

> **Authority** means having power or control over something.
>
> **Delegation** is the passing down of authority to more junior employees.

Managers

Managers are employees responsible for the day-to-day operation of the business. They work towards achieving the targets set by the owners.

Characteristics of managers

- **Authority**. They have authority over those below them.
- **Decision making**. Managers make decisions on how the targets can be met.
- **Skills and qualities**. They may have gained qualifications before being employed by the business and during training with the business. They may have experience gained from working as supervisors.
- **Delegation**. Responsibilities for less important issues can be passed to supervisors.
- **Pay and benefits**. Managers will receive salaries based on skills, responsibilities and performance.

Supervisors

Supervisors take instructions from the managers and help to ensure that the instructions are carried out by those producing the goods and services.

Characteristics of supervisors

- **Authority**. They have control over the work of the operatives.
- **Decision making**. Supervisors will make decisions about production issues as they arise.
- **Skills and qualities**. These may have had promotion from being operatives.
- **Delegation**. Some tasks may be passed to experienced operatives.
- **Pay and benefits**. Responsibilities for leading operatives will be rewarded with higher pay.

Operatives

Operatives are the workers producing the goods in factories or selling the goods in shops or carrying out clerical duties in offices.

Characteristics of operatives

- **Authority**. They have no authority within the business.
- **Decision making**. Operatives carry out the tasks set for them.
- **Skills and qualities**. Some will be fully skilled in the workplace whereas others will be partly skilled and are considered to be semi-skilled, while others will be unskilled.
- **Delegation**. There is no scope to delegate to others.
- **Pay and benefits**. Usually paid wages, operatives are the lowest paid worker, but this can increase with greater skills and experience.

Now test yourself

TESTED

1 Why is it impossible for the owners of a public limited company to control such businesses?
2 Who do business managers (a) receive their instructions from and (b) pass instructions to?
3 Why do supervisors usually understand the work and roles of operatives?
4 Why might operatives feel that they have no input into the decisions made by businesses?

Types of organisational structures

Businesses are organised as hierarchies, so control passes from the owners down through the levels to the operatives: this involves a **chain of command** from the top downwards. To be effective, leaders need to be able to pass ideas downwards and to receive feedback upwards throughout the business. This is known as a **communication pathway**.

At each level managers and supervisors will have direct control of a number of workers: this is the **span of control**. This means that employees on the next level down report to a particular manager.

Within businesses the two primary organisational structures are **tall** (sometimes known as 'hierarchical') and **flat** (sometimes known as 'horizontal').

> A **chain of command** is the line of authority within a business along which communication passes.
>
> The **span of control** is the number of employees managed directly by another employee.
>
> **Levels of hierarchy** are the layers of authority within a business.

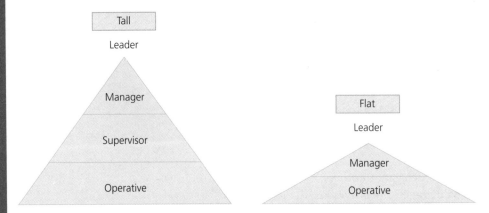

Figure 6.1 Tall and flat organisational structures

- A tall organisational structure has several **levels of hierarchy** from the top to the bottom. It involves:
  - **job roles**. There are many managers and supervisors.
  - **span of control**. Each leader, manager and supervisor controls a small number of workers.
  - **chain of command**. This has a long chain between the leaders and the operatives.
  - **communication pathway**. This tends to be long, passing through the levels. Communications take some time between top and bottom and there is some scope for misinterpretation and misunderstandings.

Evaluation of tall organisational structures

Benefits	Problems
• Managers will have a limited workload. • There can be promotion between levels, which can motivate workers.	• Communications may be slow between the levels although greater use of emails and social media can reduce the problem. • Misunderstandings may occur due to poor communication. • Decisions are carried out slowly as they are passed between the levels.

- A flat organisational structure has fewer levels of hierarchy from top to bottom. Taking out levels is known as **delayering**. Flat structures involve:
  ○ **job roles**. There are fewer managers and supervisors.
  ○ **span of control**. Each leader, manager and supervisor controls more workers.
  ○ **chain of command**. This structure will have a shorter chain between leaders and operatives.
  ○ **communication pathway**. This is shorter than that in tall structures so communication can be more rapid. Misinterpretations are reduced and misunderstandings can be quickly sorted out.

Evaluation of flat organisational structures

Benefits	Problems
• Fewer managers are needed, so costs will be reduced. • Junior managers are motivated by the greater responsibilities. • Communications are improved as messages and decisions pass through fewer levels.	• Managers have a greater span of control. • Workloads are increased at each level. • Training costs for junior managers will increase.

The type of organisational structure used by businesses will depend upon:

- **the size of the business**. Large businesses will use tall structures where roles are clearly laid out. Smaller businesses operate in flatter structures as the managers perform more jobs.
- **the aims of the business**. Those aiming at quality control at all stages will have tall structures while those aiming to keep costs down will have flatter structures.
- **management style**. Businesses aiming to have tight control over employees will have tall structures. Flat structures are used by businesses, with the **delegation** of tasks to lower ranked managers.
- **the market in which the business operates**. In the more competitive markets, costs will need to be minimised, so structures tend to be flatter.

Now test yourself

TESTED

1 What is meant by span of control?
2 In which organisational structure are managers likely to have greater responsibilities?
3 How will reducing the number of layers lead to more delegation in businesses?
4 What effect will delayering its organisational structure have on the costs of a business?

Different organisational structures

Though every business operates using a hierarchy, organisations can be structured in a number of different ways.

Function or department

Many businesses allocate people and their job roles into departments that carry out particular tasks or functions. Each department is focused on a different product or service and functions as an individual unit within the company.

> **Note**
>
> The role and functions of departments are outlined in Chapter 1.

Figure 6.2 Departmental structures

Evaluation of departmental structures

Benefits	Problems
• Employees are expert in their areas. • There is a clear chain of command. • Employees understand their roles.	• Some departments may not realise that they must work with others, so … • Co-ordination between departments may become difficult. • Departments may become resistant to changes within the business.

Product

Some businesses produce a variety of products, so they will have separate structures for each of the products manufactured. Within each of these, they are likely to be organised by function.

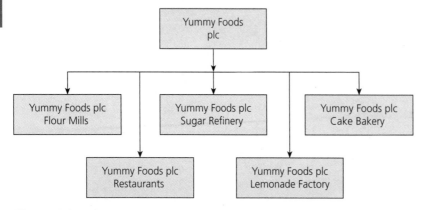

Figure 6.3 Product-based structures

Evaluation of product-based structures

Benefits	Problems
● Employees will be more able to meet customer needs for individual products. ● Employees will be experts in specific products. ● Competition between employees in different areas can be encouraged to promote sales and growth.	● There may be duplication, with each product having identical departments. ● There may be a lack of control by the leaders of the business over the production of products.

Geography

Multinational businesses will want structures based in the countries in which they operate. Similarly, businesses may have regional structures within a country. This organisational structure particularly suits businesses that need to be close to sources of supply and customers, such as retail, hospitality and transportation. Within each area workers are likely to be organised by function.

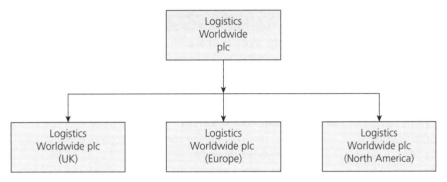

Figure 6.4 Geographical structures

Evaluation of geographical structures

Benefits	Problems
● Local customers are easier to contact, so … ● Local needs can be met. ● Local workers generally work well together, rather than being accountable to distant managers.	● Jobs, resources and functions may be repeated in each geographical area. ● Economies of scale may be lost as individual offices run themselves.

Now test yourself

TESTED

1 How will businesses gain from organising in a departmental structure?
2 Why might a product-based structure be wasteful?
3 How do businesses benefit from organising in specific geographical areas?
4 Why do product and geographic structures also use departmental structures?

Communication in the workplace

Managers and workers in businesses need to communicate with others involved in the business. Messages can be sent in a written or spoken form using traditional methods such as post and telephone, and using developments in information technology. **Communication** may involve:

- **internal communication**, where instructions and requests for information are passed downwards between leaders and operatives and responses are returned upwards
- **external communication**, where messages are passed between the business and its customers and suppliers.

> **Communication** is the exchange of information between two or more people.
>
> **Feedback** is the response stage of the communication process.

Communication needs to be effective. For this to happen it needs to be:

- accurate, so the receiver can be confident about the message
- clear, to avoid misunderstanding
- understandable by not being full of numbers or technical terms
- sent at the appropriate time so the receiver can respond.

Benefits	Problems
• **Increased employee involvement**. Workers know what is going on in the workplace. They want to be aware of decisions that affect their workplace and jobs, and be able to communicate their feelings to those above. • **Improved motivation**. Workers want to know that their efforts are appreciated by owners and managers. Also, effective communication allows workers to feel part of the business when information flows down to them. • **Working towards the same aims and objectives**. Workers need to know the targets set by their managers. • **Aids decision making**. Leaders and managers determine the objectives of the business. Before plans are put into practice, consulting with employees will help to show whether these are likely to succeed. • **Enables employee feedback**. Effective communication is not one way. Responses about operations and plans need to be made by all employees and be considered by management.	• **Low employee morale**. Workers do not like not knowing what is going on in the business. Poor communication can lead to rumours and misunderstandings, so that workers become dissatisfied with their jobs. • **Increased absenteeism**. When workers are not happy in the workplace they are more likely to stay away from work because of health issues or lack of motivation. This will affect those workers still in work and the output of the business. • **Reduced employee cooperation**. When workers have not been informed of developments in the workplace they are more likely to resist changes in practices or the introduction of new products. • **Incomplete actions and activities**. Poor communication means that workers are not clear about how jobs are to be carried out. This means that poor quality goods are being produced or work is not completed. • **Reduced efficiency**. Bad communication can lead to misunderstandings. Sorting these out can lead to production being halted.

Now test yourself

1 Where does internal communication take place?
2 What effect would communication that is not clear have on the suppliers to a business?
3 How does good communication between managers and operatives motivate workers?
4 How is the quality of products affected by bad communication?

Developing working practices

New working practices include flexible hours, home working, job sharing and zero hours contracts.

Flexible hours

With **flexible hours**, employees can work hours to suit their needs, so can start and finish work earlier and later than others.

> **Flexible hours** allow employees the chance to work at different times to suit their individual needs.

Benefits	Problems
● Workers are more motivated as they fit work around family life. ● Businesses will have workers available for longer hours. ● Employees may combine extra hours worked to take days off.	● The system is difficult to use when workers are not available during factory hours. ● Customers may find it difficult to contact workers.

Home working

Workers can work at home for part or all the week. Developments in information technology have made this much easier, and more common.

Benefits	Problems
● Businesses can have smaller workplaces, thereby saving costs. ● Workers do not have the stress of travelling to work. ● Employees can work their own hours, as long as the work is completed. ● Workers have more time at home for family commitments.	● Workers may be too easily distracted from their work. ● Workers may lose the contact with fellow workers, which is important for motivation. ● Employees may not be available for customers attempting to contact them.

Job sharing

Job sharing occurs when a job is carried out by two or more people working on selected days.

> A **job share** exists when two or more employees agree to share the responsibilities of a single job.

Benefits	Problems
● Employees will have more time at home for family commitments. ● Employers will benefit from having workers with different skills doing a job.	● Workers will need to communicate with each other to discuss the work done. ● Customers may be confused by dealing with different workers over an issue.

Zero hours contracts

Workers on **zero hours contracts** do not have a fixed number of hours to work. Some weeks they will have no hours, others they may be working full time. Workers are paid for the hours worked.

> A **zero hours contract** allows employers to hire staff without any guaranteed hours of work.

Benefits	Problems
• Businesses do not have to pay employees when no work is available. • Employees who are not available full time appreciate the ability to work occasionally.	• Some workers may be reluctant to turn down work in case they are not asked again. • Employees will not receive a regular income, so it will be difficult to pay bills.

Whether businesses adopt any of these practices will depend upon:

- **the size of the business**. Large businesses are more likely to adopt flexible hours, but smaller businesses can only operate during set opening hours.
- **the aims of the business**. Home working allows businesses to save costs by reducing the amount of office space. Large businesses can bear the costs of job sharing.
- **management style**. Managers who like to have control over employees will be more likely to use zero hours contracts. Those who do not wish to control employees closely will be comfortable with home working.
- **the market in which the business operates**. Where demand changes often, businesses are more likely to use zero hours contracts.

Now test yourself

TESTED

1 How do flexible hours help working parents?
2 Which types of workers are most suited to home working?
3 Suggest a type of business where a zero hours contract would be suitable.
4 Which practices are likely to (a) add to or (b) reduce costs for businesses?

Trade unions

Note

This topic is included in the Eduqas Specification but not in the WJEC Specification.

Note

There is no need to have detailed knowledge of the operation or organisation of trade unions.

A **trade union**, representing lots of employees, is better placed to negotiate with employers than a single employee would be. This is sometimes known as **collective bargaining**. About a quarter of the workers in Britain belong to a trade union. The main areas of negotiating involve improving:

- **Pay**

  Rates of pay tend to be higher for union members than for non-union workers due to collective bargaining. The gap between the pay of union and non-union members is known as the **trade union premium**. This shows the success of unions in working for their members.

- **Working conditions**

  Unions will negotiate with employers on such issues as:
  - **working hours**, for example how long they should be and when they should be worked. This may include overtime and shift patterns.
  - **new working practices**, for example flexible working and zero hours contracts.
  - the amount of paid **holiday** workers should be entitled to.
  - the **facilities** available in the workplace, for example restrooms and eating space.
  - **health and safety** concerns with regards to dangerous working conditions and issues such as temperatures in the workplace.

Generally, trade union negotiations are enough to settle differences between the workers and their employers. When they are not, unions take **industrial action**.

Types of industrial action

- **Overtime bans**, where workers just work for their set hours. This may make it difficult for businesses to complete orders, and so perhaps lose contracts.
- **Go-slows**, meaning fewer goods are produced.
- **Strike action**, when workers refuse to go to work. Legally, a ballot of union members must be held and 50 per cent of those voting must agree to a strike before it can take place. Advance notice must also be given to employers so they can make arrangements within the workplace and let suppliers and customers know.

Overtime bans and **go-slows** aim to persuade an employer to settle an industrial dispute before it goes any further. Workers will continue to be paid, but the output of businesses will be reduced. Strikes are a last resort for workers as, during the dispute, they lose their pay and their employers lose output. Striking trade unions, and their members, can picket outside their place of work to protest, and also try to persuade others to join the strike.

A **trade union** is a group of people who work together to improve their pay and working conditions.

The **trade union wage premium** is the difference in wages paid to union members and non-union members for doing similar jobs.

Industrial action is any activity organised by employees or trade unions as part of a protest against an employer during a dispute.

A **go-slow** occurs when employees work more slowly and with less effort than is normal.

Now test yourself

1 Why are trade unions more likely to gain wage increases than individual workers?
2 Besides better pay, what do trade unions attempt to gain for their members?
3 How do go-slows affect businesses?
4 Why are strikes a last resort for trade union members?

Exam practice questions

Exam practice: *Business activity*

The retirement of the previous owner has led Carolyn John to be made redundant from a local shop selling gifts to tourists. She had worked at the shop for over ten years and had learned many skills in the shop and in the office. In her area there are fairly high levels of unemployment so her chances of finding another job are limited. Carolyn decided to use her savings and a bank loan to buy the shop. To obtain the loan she had to draw up a business plan for the bank.

She knew that there were risks involved as in her area she found that 1800 businesses had been set up the previous year but, in the same year, 1200 had closed.

The business has survived for two years of Carolyn's ownership, but she felt that it could do better by expanding to a larger shop. She is considering taking on a partner to enable her to do this.

(a) What term describes the type of ownership Carolyn has before taking on a partner? [1]
(b) Carolyn will have unlimited liability. What does this mean for businesses such as Carolyn's? [2]
(c) Apart from the description of the business and of its owners, suggest three types of information banks would consider important in a business plan. [3]
(d) The bank will look closely at the likely success of Carolyn's business including the percentage of businesses that have closed to the number of start-ups. Calculate that percentage. [2]
(e) Carolyn could be described as an entrepreneur. Outline two characteristics of being an entrepreneur. [4]
(f) Advise Carolyn on whether taking on a partner would be a good idea for her and the business. [8]

ONLINE

Exam practice: *Influences on business*

Patio Paths Co Ltd replaces driveways and paths at customers' houses. They have branches throughout the United Kingdom, employing 500 workers. In all, 100 of the workers are employed in the offices and the rest are manual workers building driveways.

The business is a very much up to date in its use of IT in dealing with its stakeholders.

Over the years they have developed their own designs and methods for constructing driveways. Patio Paths Co Ltd feels that it needs to legally protect their designs and methods.

Success in the United Kingdom has meant that Patio Paths Co Ltd is considering opening branches in other countries.

(a) Suggest an IT package that businesses could introduce to improve their administration in:
    (i) completing their accounts
    (ii) finding customers' telephone numbers
    (iii) contacting customers to remind them to pay their accounts. [3]
(b) Outline:
    (i) one legal responsibility Patio Paths Co Ltd have to their customers
    (ii) one legal responsibility they have to their employees. [4]
(c) Calculate the percentage of Patio Paths Co Ltd workers who are employed building driveways, [2]
(d) What effect might each of the following have on Patio Paths Co Ltd's business?
    (i) A cut in the rate of income tax paid by Patio Paths Co Ltd's customers.
    (ii) An increase in the rate of interest paid on Patio Paths Co Ltd's bank loan. [2]
(e) Why do businesses need to be able to protect their intellectual property? [1]
(f) Discuss whether Patio Paths Co Ltd should set up branches in other countries. [8]

ONLINE

Exam practice: *Business operations*

Pacckers Ltd have been producing packaging material for the food industry for many years. During this time they have used traditional methods of stock control, but now they are considering JIT.

The customers of the business buy large quantities of paper and plastic boxes in a variety of shapes and sizes.

Pacckers Ltd have carried out research to find out whether customers are satisfied with the quality of products supplied by the business. The research asked 200 customers their opinions. The table below shows some of the results from the research.

Satisfaction	
Totally satisfied	134
Usually satisfied	42
Totally dissatisfied	24

(a) What two types of stock are Pacckers Ltd likely to hold? [2]

(b) Which method of production are Pacckers Ltd likely to use in producing their goods? Explain your answer. [4]

(c) Identify three pieces of information firms such as Pacckers Ltd will need during the procurement process. [3]

(d) Calculate the percentage of customers of Pacckers Ltd who were not totally satisfied with the products supplied. [3]

(e) Advise Pacckers Ltd on whether they should adopt just in time in the production process. [8]

ONLINE

Exam practice: *Finance*

EMQ plc is a printing business that produces brochures and reports for multinational companies, programmes for sporting and theatrical events, and a variety of magazines. Its latest annual report for shareholders included the following profit and loss account. The directors are not pleased with the results as net profit had fallen and was now below target.

They are hopeful of future improvements after an increase in the number of orders so, despite the profit situation, EMQ plc is considering buying new machinery.

Profit and loss account: EMQ plc		
	This year (£ million)	Last year (£ million)
Turnover	6.8	6.0
Cost of sales	3.3	2.8
Gross profit	3.5	3.2
Expenses	1.8	1.4
Net profit	1.7	1.8

(a) What is meant by the term turnover as used in the profit and loss accounts shown above? [2]

(b) Calculate the net profit margin earned by EMQ plc for this year. (Show your workings.) [2]

(c) Outline two sources of finance businesses such as EMQ plc could use to buy new machinery. [4]

(d) Despite the worse than expected profits EMQ plc have a healthy cash flow.
  (i) What is meant by the term cash flow? [2]
  (ii) Why are cash-flow forecasts important to (a) the managers and (b) the workers in a business? [2]

(e) Advise on the ways in which the directors could attempt to increase profits in the future. [8]

ONLINE

Exam practice: *Marketing*

Despite being the only theatre for many miles, Stages Theatre has had disappointing ticket sales. The theatre is in a small market town and is owned by a co-operative of theatre goers. They have decided to carry out market research to find what can be done to increase the size of its audiences.

The market research showed that many in the area did not know about the shows being put on by the theatre. The managers are considering how they can correct this situation.

(a) Describe two types of market research Stages Theatre could use.   [4]
(b) What is meant by unique selling point (USP)? What is the USP of Stages Theatre?   [2]
(c) Describe a pricing strategy you recommend in each of the following situations. Give reasons
     for your answers.
     (i) The managers of the theatre are happy to make a small profit just above costs.
     (ii) The managers want to increase the number of older customers it has for afternoon shows.   [4]
(d) Why is the brand Stages Theatre important to this business?   [2]
(e) Advise the managers of Stages Theatre on the media they could use to promote the theatre
     and increase sales.   [8]

ONLINE ☐

Exam practice: *Human resources*

Iota Technologies Ltd have received an order from a major supermarket. This has meant that they plan to expand their factory, employ more workers and reorganise various departments within the business.

Training of existing and new workers will be needed to meet the development in the business.

(a) Briefly describe the importance of the following in the recruitment process.
     (i) the job description
     (ii) references.   [4]
(b) Why is it important for businesses to have a well-motivated workforce?   [2]
(c) Outline two non-financial methods Iota Technologies Ltd could use to motivate their workers to
     increase output to help meet the order.   [4]
(d) Iota Technologies Ltd are planning to reorganise their departmental system from having a tall
     structure to a flatter structure. Outline one advantage businesses gain from doing so.   [2]
(e) Advise Iota Technologies Ltd on whether they should use just on-the-job training to prepare the
     workers and recruits.   [8]

ONLINE ☐

Notes

Now test yourself and exam practice answers at **www.hoddereducation.co.uk/myrevisionnotesdownloads**